THE SUNDAY *after* THE FUNERAL

TIMOTHY S. THOMPSON

WESTBOW
PRESS®

A DIVISION OF THOMAS NELSON
& ZONDERVAN

WestBow Press books may be ordered through booksellers or by contacting:

WestBow Press
A Division of Thomas Nelson & Zondervan
1663 Liberty Drive
Bloomington, IN 47403
www.westbowpress.com
1 (866) 928-1240

All scripture quotations are taken from the King James Version copyright 2017.

ISBN: 978-1-9736-9671-1 (sc)
ISBN: 978-1-9736-9670-4 (hc)
ISBN: 978-1-9736-9672-8 (e)

Library of Congress Control Number: 2020912720

Print information available on the last page.

WestBow Press rev. date: 7/23/2020

CONTENTS

LIST OF TABLES

VERSION STATEMENT

Unless otherwise noted all Biblical quotations
are taken from the Holy Bible, King James Version
of the Holy Bible, Christian Art Publishers, 2017

ACKNOWLEDGEMENTS

First, I want to express praise and adoration to the Lord Jesus Christ for the enabling and inspiration to embark upon this effort. My prayer is that this project will bless those who read it in the future and that this project will contribute to the furthering of the Kingdom of Heaven on earth.

Second, I want to express my deepest love and appreciation to my Wife, Tamra. Baby, I am grateful to you for your encouragement, support, and assistance in creating this project. I thank God for you.

Third, I want to express gratitude to all of the pastors I interviewed for their support in sharing in their stories with me.

Finally, I want to express gratitude to my dissertation committee. Dr. John Harvey, Dr. Andre Rogers, and Dr. Bryan Bohlman, thank you for your guidance and support throughout the writing process.

ABSTRACT

This research set out to examine preaching as a modality of pastoral care for congregations that have experienced deaths resulting from traumatic events. Using the qualitative approach, the research employed the phenomenological strategy. In this particular case, the phenomenon involved pastors who provided pastoral through preaching care for congregations that suffered deaths resulting from traumas. The primary means through which I personally engaged local church pastors was interviews. During the study, I closely examined three types of traumas: homicides, suicides, and tragic deaths. After that, I interviewed two pastors from each category. A total of six pastors, subsequently, participated in the study.

In the process, I gave pastors full liberties to share their stories in the manners they deemed appropriate. Then, the respondents' data were presented through homiletic strategies, homiletic intervention dynamics, and homiletic directions. First, the homiletic strategies explored pastoral involvement, homiletic strategy components, listening to the Holy Spirit, and primacy of preaching. Second, the homiletic intervention dynamics studied the dominant preaching themes and major tasks while engaging grief following traumatic deaths. Third, homiletic directions included homiletic campaigns and various homiletic approaches of each pastor when ministering to grieving congregations.

Furthermore, I made sure that all of the interviews did not manipulate information in any way. This decision was to ensure the protection of the privacy of certain pieces of information. The findings presented fascinating results which seemed appropriate for other pastors. This researcher, therefore, anticipates further studies in other crucial areas of related homiletics.

CHAPTER 1

The focus of this research is to examine preaching as a modality of pastoral care. In particular, it will study preaching as pastoral care to a grieving congregation following a tragic loss. Pastoral ministry, research reveals, is a multifaceted discipline that consists of various ministry practices. One of these practices is homiletics. This project, then, seeks to understand how preaching ministers to a traumatized congregation. Accordingly, preaching is treated as one of those means of pastoral ministry. Moving forward, chapter 1 establishes the purpose of this study and also addresses research questions, disciplines, limitations, challenges, and explanation of the research.

Tragic losses are often traumatizing to individuals, families, congregations, and communities as a whole. This study approaches pastoral preaching with sensitivity to the psychological, emotional, physical, and spiritual needs of those traumatized. The research will examine four contextual areas that define the parameters of this study. They are denominational, congregational, geographical, and professional.

In terms of denominational context, research focuses primarily on one religious body, the Southern Baptist Convention. There are various reasons for focusing on one religious body as opposed to different religious bodies. First, it narrows the research without unnecessary complexity. Second, denominational connections necessary to field research are already in place. These connections make the field research more achievable. Third, studying more than one denomination complicates the process due to theological differences. The project will therefore focus on only one denomination. Regarding congregational context, this study emphasizes public ministry as opposed to individual-based ministry. This research looks at ministry to a congregation that is in the throes of a traumatic loss. The ministry of preaching takes on different approaches, depending on circumstances and liturgical calendar. This particular study on preaching targets ministry as it pertains to congregations that are grieving after a tragic loss. This type of preaching is situation-oriented rather than liturgical or seasonal.

The other side to the congregational context is the format. Sermons that are usually delivered to grieving congregations are done in the format of funeral messages. This research, however, accentuates pastoral messages delivered to congregations following the funeral. Moreover, it is also concerned with the pastoral and theological depth of these messages.

The professional context is another dynamic of this study. Pastors for congregations and associate pastors who have preaching roles make up the professional context of this project. In some churches, the senior pastor is the individual who assumes all preaching responsibilities. In other churches, associates help in the preaching ministry.

This project, consequently, is written with preaching pastors in mind, regardless of their official positions. Professionals other than pastors also often preach to grieving congregations. Some of these other professionals are chaplains, bishops, association directors, and district superintendents. In some cases, these other professionals pastor churches where they have regular preaching responsibilities. These professionals are also included in the professional context, in order to enrich its informational benefit.

Finally, there is the geographical context. Traumas occur all over the country. These traumas also affect churches, as is reported almost daily in the media. This study, however, examines only churches in South Carolina. More specifically, it looks primarily at congregations in the Midlands and the upper state. Narrowing the focus in this way makes the research field more manageable.

CONSULTING THE DISCIPLINES

The aforementioned parameters will incorporate information gathered from various necessary disciplines such as theology, homiletics, psychology, and sociology. Since the topic of the research is multifaceted, these disciplines serve as target areas of study. A review of sources relative to this study reveals a scarcity of current information. Therefore, information for this research will derive from the most reliable and current sources available.

Since theology is a necessary discipline for this study, the field of pastoral theology is the primary focus. Pastoral theology is essentially the branch of theology that studies systematic principles and theories of pastoral care. Moreover, since the core of this research is theological in nature, it will emphasize the practical side of theology.

The next discipline is homiletics. Homiletics centers on the style, structure, and delivery of sermons. This research, as such, examines homiletics from the perspective of how pastors care for grieving congregations through preaching. This exercise in homiletics is often described as pastoral preaching. In order to add balance to the research, this study will also examine several preaching theories and then challenge them at different levels. This process provides a balanced understanding of the effectiveness of pastoral preaching.

Another discipline important to this study is psychology. It is important to note, however, that this research emphasizes psychology from the perspective of Christianity. The purpose for researching psychology is that psychology and theology intersect one another when studying pastoral preaching. This study seeks to demonstrate how psychology from a Christian perspective also informs pastoral preaching.

The final discipline important to this research is sociology. In particular, this research will examine sociological studies by national and state agencies that relate to tragic events. Sociological data of this type gathered from various agencies is critical in establishing the foundation for pastoral preaching. The researcher will accordingly present statistical information that undergirds the necessity of preaching that comforts the grieving.

EXPLAINING THE BACKGROUND

As stated briefly, this research looks at the effectiveness of preaching as a means of pastoral care to grieving congregations. Essentially, this topic derives from my own personal experiences which that have inspired me to embark upon this study. They include tragic events that have radically reshaped the author's pastoral ministry. This section will, therefore, describe some events that inspired the author to embark upon this journey.

The summer of 2009 is forever etched in the author's memory. It involves a congregation of about ninety parishioners in Johnston, South Carolina. Throughout the previous two years, many families joined the congregation. The fervor in worship in the service was increasing, and the congregation was growing. Though already members of the church, a particular family had been inactive for a while but then returned to church and began to attend more regularly. They seemed like a happy couple. Nothing seemed out of the ordinary.

One evening, a distraught parishioner contacted the pastor. The pastor answered the phone and received the news that someone in the congregation had died tragically. Without hesitation, the pastor rushed to the family's home, entering an emotionally charged scene. Family members were huddled around each other, all of them appearing to be horrified. After a few minutes, a church member approached the pastor and took him to the family. She introduced him to those in the family who did not know him.

The deceased's wife then unfolded the tragic account of her beloved husband's untimely demise. She described how she found him in the backyard, lying in a pool of blood, with a shotgun lying next to him. As she related those details, she began to sob loudly. Another church member rushed to the wife's side to console her. Over the next several hours, the pastor provided as much support as was possible given the circumstances.

In the days ahead, family members from all over the state gathered for the viewing and funeral. The funeral was awkward and difficult. Then the pastor prepared for the regular worship service. On the Sunday morning following the funeral, the pastor spoke to the youth during Sunday school. Before the class even began, more people entered the room. Interestingly, all the newcomers were adults. Then, more people walked in until a class that usually had ten members now numbered almost thirty attendees. Everyone asked painful and difficult questions about suicide and the deceased church member's spiritual status. Discovering that this situation was a pastoral moment, the pastor engaged in support-oriented dialogue.

When the worship hour arrived, the pastor sought God once more for direction. Stepping behind the pulpit, the pastor faced a confused and saddened congregation. He preached a sermon for which there were no precedents. The title of the pastor's sermon was "Your Life Is Worth Living."

Memorial Day weekend of 2012 was also unforgettable. This event involved a small congregation in Rock Hill, South Carolina. When the phone rang, the pastor answered to hear an emotionally shaken parishioner on the other end with some tragic news. It sounded all too familiar, although the circumstances were different this time.

The news involved a much-loved parishioner. He and his son were working on the father's farm, moving a grain auger. It was a laborious operation, requiring two people to move the device. While moving the auger, the two men inadvertently hit a high-tension line overhead. Immediately, thousands of volts entered the son's body, killing him almost instantly. The father, meanwhile, was severely injured from electrical burns. He was immediately flown to the burn center in Augusta, Georgia.

The rest of the week involved numerous six-hour round trips to the burn center in Georgia. A desperate family greeted the pastor each day when he arrived. Back at home, the pastor visited other parishioners, who were burdened with grief. The following week, the funeral took place. The entire family was devastated.

People from all over the state attended the funeral. Each person was stricken with disbelief and felt deeply perplexed. Some of the people asked why God would allow such a tragedy to happen to people they loved. Others simply tried to resign themselves to the will of an all-wise God. Everyone felt the same feeling of grief, but none of them felt this grief more profoundly than the family.

Dreading the worship service that was rapidly approaching, the pastor prayed again for divine direction. On the morning of the service, the pastor faced yet another saddened and shocked crowd of people—but he did feel a bit more prepared this time. He opened his Bible and introduced his message. The congregation sat in silence.

The pastor still felt uneasy and ill equipped, despite previous similar experiences. Expressions of sadness and despair shadowed the faces of the parishioners. The pastor then engaged in what seemed more like a monologue from the Bible than a typical sermon. A deep bond formed between the congregation and the pastor throughout the event. It was an event wherein the mourner was comforting the grieving.

Some conclusions come to mind. First, the loss of life affects everyone else in a congregation. This cause-and-effect process means that people's lives are intertwined with each other. In fact, 1 Corinthians 12:26 reinforces this thought. Paul writes, "And if one member suffers, all the members suffer with it; or if one member is honored, all the members rejoice with it."

Second, grief does not end with the funeral. This realization became quite clear in both instances. Grief support is necessary even after the funeral. In fact, J. Randall Nichols described the necessity of post funeral pastoral preaching. He explained,

> Preaching in a loss situation is a seed sowing process. Someday parts of what we say may strike root in new understanding and perception. It is not so much that the content of what we say in a given sermon will itself be remembered but rather that we introduce people even in their distraughtness to a different way of seeing things. We begin a restorative, reconstructive process whose outcome will look very different from anything we might picture at the start of it. The important thing is that it is begun and that we all know it. [1]

What is more, grief support includes, but does not end with,

---

[1] J. Randall Nichols. *The Restoring Word: Preaching as Pastoral Communication* (San Francisco: Harper and Row Publications, 1987): 57.

pastoral visits. This grief process also means that ministry through the Word is necessary.

Third, pastoral visits are excellent opportunities to gauge people's grieving processes. Pastoral visits in both instances proved to be invaluable sources of information in gauging the emotional status of members. In fact, pastoral visits helped contribute to the direction and depth of the sermon on the Sunday following the funeral.

Fourth, these experiences are universal, meaning that other ministers have experienced similar ministry situations. This realization, therefore, compelled this writer to search for ways these lessons might benefit others.

Finally, there must be a connection between what is happening in people's lives and what occurs in the pulpit. In situations such as those described above, the pastor must connect the Sunday morning sermon with the tragedy. This connection is possible only through preaching truth and grace to a shattered community. The pastor potentially misses an opportunity to minister effectively if parish life and Sunday preaching are disconnected.

Preaching grace and truth is indispensable to the pastor's role in the local church. Even so, this call to preach does not supersede other areas of ministry; it complements them. A ministry of presence with hurting parishioners is essential. Preaching the Word of God, however, is equally essential. This principle is especially true when tragedy strikes a local church. Pastoral ministry amid tragic events not only defines but also substantiates the pastor's role in the local congregation.

ASKING THE RIGHT QUESTIONS

Certain research questions for this particular study are necessary. Functionally, research questions serve two purposes. First, they narrow the focus of the research problem and are stated in open-ended terms. Second, they address more specific areas of the empirical unknown, which are based on field research.[2] The following research questions will guide the current study.

- How do the preacher's theological convictions inform the task of preaching to traumatized congregations?
- How is preaching the Word of God important to pastoral care for grieving congregations?
- How does the scriptural mandate to preach inform the task of preaching to grieving congregations?
- How does the preacher's heart attitude make preaching to grieving congregations effective?
- How is the task of preaching different from other ways of providing pastoral care to a grieving congregation?

ESTABLISHING SOME GUIDELINES

I established clear and definitive delimitations in order to make the research more manageable. By that I essentially mean self-imposed guidelines that narrow the research field and provide direction.[3] Four delimitations apply to this study. First, the majority of the

---

[2] John C. Cresswell. *Qualitative Inquiry and Research Design.* (Thousand Oaks: SAGE Publishers, 2013): 23.

[3] George Largan. *PHDStudent.com.* January 1, 2017. http://www.phdstudent.com (accessed March 1, 2017).

sources consulted for this research relate to post-funeral preaching. The reason for this delimitation is that funeral and Sunday morning messages have different emphases. For instance, books about funeral messages typically guide the reader in constructing the entire funeral service. Much of this information, however, is not appropriate to Sunday worship services.

Second, the group chosen for this research is pastors of local churches. Local pastors are embedded in local congregations. This closeness accordingly allows pastors to engage members on a daily basis. Moreover, this type of connection is conducive to more intimate knowledge of people's needs. This pastoral relationship also sets them apart from other professionals like superintendents, bishops, and directors of missions.

Third, Southern Baptists are the target population. Although pastoral ministry is similar for all denominations, theology is often the variable. Some faiths, therefore, approach soteriology, hamartiology, and Christology differently than Southern Baptists. These differences affect how pastors approach preaching and pastoral care. In addition, some ministers of some faith groups do not engage in cross-denominational dialogue. This disengagement, in turn, affects the reporting process of the information. The research process, therefore, is more easily managed by focusing on Southern Baptists.

Fourth, the pastors of churches in the upstate region of South Carolina are the target group for this research for several reasons. Traveling, for example, to the coastal regions is time-consuming and costly. Moreover, concentrating on congregations of the Midlands and Piedmont regions narrows the research. Also, communication with ministers in these regions is easier to manage for the purposes of the research. Finally, personal interviews are preferred for the research process. Interviews are therefore more practical if research is conducted in these regions.

Finally, another delimitation of the research process is the specific target group within the pastoral vocation. The research will focus primarily on solo-paid pastors of local congregations. That said the target group will include full-time or bi-vocational pastors. The vast majority of congregations in the Southern Baptist Convention are between forty and one hundred members. Research, therefore, will include six Southern Baptist congregations of forty to four hundred and fifty members that have experienced congregational loss. In addition, grief levels vary according to the type of trauma people have experienced. Accordingly, the study will concentrate on two congregations from each of the following traumatic events: suicide, tragic death, and homicide.

IDENTIFYING THE OBSTACLES

There are four possible challenges to researching this topic. One possible challenge is the pastors' willingness to be interviewed. Some ministers prefer not to talk about their experiences to others whom they do not know. The next challenge is contacting appropriate ministers. The researcher faces the task of finding contacts. Another challenge is the potential lack of responses to questionnaires. Some ministers are not willing to respond to questionnaires.

Coupled with this challenge is the timeliness of survey responses from the ministers. Procrastination of responses is a possible factor affecting the field of research. A fourth challenge is the number of pastors with experience in this type of intervention, in light of varying experiences and pastoral ministry styles. The researcher will make necessary adjustments throughout the process as challenges present themselves.

WHY THIS BOOK IS IMPORTANT

This section essentially examines how preaching as pastoral care in times of tragic loss is important for other pastors. First, research reveals few resources that specifically address preaching as pastoral care. Not only are resources scarce, but there is little scholarly research that addresses an important growing need.

Resources that speak to sermon preparation, sermon outlines, seasonal sermons, and funeral sermons are plentiful. These resources usually occupy entire bookstore sections. Even though books on the topic of preaching as a means of pastoral care in times of tragic loss are available, they are fewer in number. In fact, they are often rare and sometimes difficult to find. This lack of necessary scholarship, then, leaves a knowledge gap. This information gap also presents a challenge to pastors who find themselves in need of such information.

This research seeks to fill this information gap in a small way. Many ministers have encountered situations such as those described above. Some of these ministers live in the general locale of the writer. This study, therefore, seeks to assist all ministers with another helpful resource.

Second, today's cultural shift embraces openness and transparency from the pulpit. Until the late twentieth century, transparency from the pulpit was not welcomed. In fact, many homiletics professors in the past often discouraged such preaching. Today, transparency is actually considered a sermonic strength. J. Kent Edwards described this homiletic barrier and then defended the value of being humanly vulnerable from the pulpit. Moreover, he declared that deep preachers are not "afraid to admit their frailties, failures and insecurities."[4] Transparency in preaching, he explained, fortifies the pastoral bond with a congregation. This research, therefore, seeks to amplify the necessity of transparency from the pulpit. It does so through addressing a tragic event and the pain of a grieving congregation through preaching.

When a congregation suffers a loss in its community, people grieve. The number of people grieving from the event includes most, if not all, of the congregation. A refreshing word of hope from the pulpit, therefore, is critical at these times. There are moments, as well, when pastors themselves feel either inadequate or too emotionally affected to engage their grieving people. What are ministers to do in such cases?

Charles Bachman, for example, teaches that pastors must first understand their own emotions. Ministers are more effective pastorally, he explains, when they understand their own emotional state before they preach. He also encourages awareness in ministers that parishioners grieve and feel some of the same emotions as the pastor. If pastors are too introspective, they weaken their sensitivities to their congregations. Nevertheless, he argues that it is incumbent upon pastors to intervene and do so effectively.[5]

---

[4] Kent J. Edwards. *Deep Preaching: Creating Sermons That Go Beyond the Superficial.* (Nashville: B & H Publishing Group, 2009): 175–176.

[5] Charles Bachman. *Ministering to the Grief Sufferer.* (Philadelphia: Fortress Press, 1964): 31.

In the section below, I will present empirical unknowns which address some major concerns about preaching based on responses during interviews. Following the empirical unknowns are research questions which speak to key issues surrounding how preaching programs are implemented and to what extent.

THE RESEARCH PROBLEM IN A NUTSHELL

Research Problem: How effective is preaching as a modality of pastoral care for a congregation that has suffered a tragic loss?

Empirical Unknown: *What is the value of preaching in providing pastoral care to a congregation that has suffered a tragic loss?*

Research Question 1: How do the preacher's theological convictions inform the task of preaching to traumatized congregations?

Empirical Unknown: *What is the extent to which preaching is utilized as a means of pastoral care?*

RQ 2: How is preaching the Word of God important to pastoral care for grieving congregations?

RQ 3: How does the scriptural mandate to preach inform the task of preaching to traumatized congregations?

Empirical Unknown: *What is the relationship between pastoral support and preaching following a tragic loss in the congregation?*

RQ 4: How does the preacher's heart attitude make preaching to traumatized congregations effective?

RQ 5: How is the task of preaching distinct from other ways of providing pastoral support to grieving congregations?

Scholarship reveals preaching to be a means of pastoral care. It is unknown, though, to what extent preachers integrate preaching into their pastoral care. The initial empirical unknown, therefore, seeks to understand its value from the perspectives of ministers. The first empirical unknown investigates how one's scriptural convictions influence preaching. It therefore asks, "How do the preacher's theological convictions inform the task of preaching to traumatized congregations?"

The second unknown is the extent to which preaching is utilized as a means of pastoral care. This second empirical unknown begins with asking, "How is preaching the Word of God important to pastoral care for grieving congregations?" Essentially, the research question examines the value of the Word of God to grieving congregations. It examines preaching of the Word versus proclaiming merely psychological principles and "feel-good" theologies.

In addition to this research question, this empirical unknown also seeks to understand "How does the scriptural mandate to preach inform the task of preaching to grieving congregations?" Scholarship reveals that preaching is not regarded as important today as it was two hundred years ago. Moreover, scholars reveal that preachers have varying opinions as to the degree of importance of preaching as it applies to pastoral care. While some ministers place great value on the task of preaching as a means of pastoral care, other ministers do not.

The third empirical unknown addresses the relationship between pastoral care and preaching. This last unknown stems from two primary research questions. First, it asks, "How does the preacher's heart attitude make preaching to traumatized congregations effective?" Years spent in local church ministry have revealed to this author that relationships between pastors and parishioners are important. Relationships are especially important when the minister is called upon to comfort a grieving congregation.

The next research question asks, "How is the task of preaching distinct from other ways of providing pastoral support to grieving congregations?" Ministers have various spiritual gifts available to them through the Holy Spirit. This research question, therefore, asks how preaching is different from counseling, scripture reading, music, and support groups.

CHAPTER 2

The motivation for researching preaching as a modality of pastoral care mainly stems from the question that pastors often ask: "How can pastors/clergy help?" Knowing exactly what to say to a grieving congregation following a traumatic loss is daunting. What is more, the lengths to which the pastor addresses such intense situations is further challenging.

Pastoral ministry is multifaceted, and preaching is a critically important facet of pastoral ministry. Moreover, preaching is arguably the core of pastoral ministry. Therefore, chapter 2 seeks to examine several nuances of preaching to a traumatized congregation based on a review of literature—specifically, the role of preaching, homiletical approach, scriptural authority, and context. Since people's lives are deeply affected by traumatic loss, relationships are likewise affected. Extensions of these relationships often include the churches that grieving people attend. These situations, then, present pastors with challenges on the Sunday morning following the funeral.

During the course of the literature review, certain themes

became apparent and determined the direction and focus of this chapter accordingly. The goal here is to examine various works to present a broader base of information. Since psychology/pastoral theology, homiletics, and sociology are core disciplines of this research, the literature review focused on these same disciplines. Availability of current scholarship on the research topic was sparse, which required research of most sources written in the latter part of the twentieth century.

Once again, this outline is based on the major themes reflected in literature research. The first part of this chapter will focus on the ministry of pastoral care. The second part will examine the ministry of pastoral preaching. Then, the third part will focus on expositional preaching as it applies to pastoral ministry. A brief paragraph of reflection will follow each section, with a conclusion at the end of the chapter.

THE MINISTRY OF PASTORAL CARE

This study begins with the ministry of pastoral care because all the contributors in the literature review began with pastoral care. Most of the scholarship, in fact, contended for a relationship between preaching and pastoral care. Research of literature also revealed that the perspectives of scholars on pastoral preaching varied. In some cases, scholarship argued that preaching was on par with pastoral care. In other cases, however, writers contended that preaching was not necessarily on par with pastoral care but was nonetheless important. Notwithstanding, the literature review also revealed that some scholars did not have a high esteem for preaching at all. Overall, though, scholars agreed that pastoral care and preaching in some fashion inform each other.

Chapter 2 will seek to accomplish three objectives. In so doing, presenting an overall picture is often helpful. Therefore, this chapter will set the stage for pastoral care—providing biblical scenes of trauma, contemporary contexts of trauma, and then a definition of trauma. Following biblical scenes and contexts of trauma, this section will establish a definitional pastoral care beginning with biblical models of pastoral care. Then, several perspectives on pastoral care from leading authors will be presented. Finally, this chapter will seek to demonstrate to the reader why pastoral care is necessary. To reiterate, the endeavor in this chapter is to lay the foundation for preaching as a modality for pastoral care.

Part 1.1 Traumas in the Bible

Biblical stories contain messages of hope, peace, and reconciliation.[6] These same messages are what pastoral care also seeks to communicate. These messages also give direction in implementing pastoral care in a congregational setting.

To start with, it is helpful to note certain instances of trauma in the Bible. Scripture not only speaks of trauma, it often depicts it through observable tragedies. The following incident is an example of an observable tragedy with unspeakable trauma. The intensity of grief is unmistakable in Matthew 2:16–18, where Herod coldly murders innocent children.

---

[6] Henry C. Thiesson. *Lectures in Systematic Theology.* (Grand Rapids: Eerdmans Publishing Company, 1989): 8–10.

"Then Herod, when he saw that he was mocked of the wise men, was exceeding wroth, and sent forth, and slew all the children that were in Bethlehem, and in all the coasts thereof, from two years old and under, according to the time which he had diligently enquired of the wise men. Then was fulfilled that which was spoken by Jeremy the prophet, saying, ' In Rama was there a voice heard, lamentation, and weeping, and great mourning, Rachel weeping for her children, and would not be comforted because they are not.'"

Here, young, innocent children paid the price for the jealousy of a man who was mentally and emotionally unstable. To Flavius Josephus, a Jewish historian, Herod was completely mad. Josephus attributes Herod's murderous actions in Matthew 2 to some type of mental illness.[7]

Another instance involves the betrayal of Joseph. His trauma unfolds in Genesis 37:25–28.

"And they sat down to eat bread; and they lifted up their eyes and looked, and, behold, a company of Ishmeelites came from Giliead with their camels bearing spicery and balm and myrrh, going to carry it down to Egypt. And Judah said unto his brethren, 'What profit is it if we slay our brethren, and conceal his blood? Come, and let us sell him to the

---

[7] William Whiston. *The New Complted Works of Josephus.* (Grand Rapids: Kregel Publications, 1999): 535.

Ishmeelites, and let not our hand be upon him' for he is our brother and our flesh.' And his brethren were content. Then there passed by Midianites merchantmen; and they drew and lifted up Joseph out of the pit, and sold Joseph to the Ishmeelites for twenty pieces of silver: and they brought Joseph into Egypt."

For simply doing what his father had instructed him to do, Joseph suddenly realized that he was the center of intense hatred. This hatred issued from a selfish and vindictive spirit in his brothers. His life was transformed that day. Joseph eventually recovered, but the central truth gleaned from these examples is that tragic events were as painful then as they are today.

Part 1.2 Traumas in the Modern Context

Traumatic deaths occur frequently and in contexts common to everyone. If nothing else, traumatic deaths are perpetual aspects of human existence. To start with, two questions launch this section into motion: *What does trauma mean?* and *How is it understood in the context of this research?*

Journey of the Hearts is a professional journal that provides online support services for those struggling with emotional trauma. One year following the attack on the World Trade Center towers, *Journey of the Hearts* published an article on the events. In it, Kristi Dyer declared that a traumatic death is "one that is sudden, unanticipated, violent, mutilating or destructive, random and/or preventable, involves multiple deaths, or is one in which the mourner has a personal encounter with death."[8] In that same article, she explained that a sudden death was different. Sudden death, she continued, occurs without warning and without apparent reason to the sufferer.

Dr. H. Norman Wright is a marriage, family, and child therapist and a certified trauma specialist. In *The New Guide to Crises and Trauma Counseling,* Wright explains the crisis situation. He writes, "One day we will encounter a change or problem that seems beyond our capacity to cope. When a problem is overwhelming or when our support system—within ourselves or from others—doesn't work, we are thrown off balance. This is called a crisis." He also contends that people should anticipate, even expect, crises to develop.

Next, Wright explains trauma. He declares that trauma is more than a crisis—it is "a normal reaction to abnormal events that overwhelm a person's abilities to adapt to life—where you feel powerless." [9] *Trauma* derives from the Greek word for *wound,* which implies the reaction to an event. Wright further clarifies that, while a crisis is an event that exceeds one's resources to cope, a trauma is the inner wound one sustains.[10]

Whether it is a traumatic death or a sudden death, the grief is often the same. Pathologists have identified four major types of

---

[8] Kristi Dyer. *Journey of the Heart.* September 11, 2002. http://www. journeyofthehearts.org (accessed June 2, 2016). In her article, Dyer explained the repercussions of the events on September 11, 2001, on the one-year anniversary.
[9] Norman H. Wright. *The New Guide to Crisis and Trauma Counseling.* (Ventura: Regal Books, 2003). In this chapter, Wright provides an overview of the different kinds of death as well as their emotional impact on page 11.
[10] Ibid., 194.

death: illness, accidental, homicide, and suicide.[11] All these deaths can be sudden as well as traumatic. Of these four types, the last two are particularly traumatic. The National Trauma Institute (NTI), for example, reported over 192,000 traumatic deaths in the United States in 2015.[12] NTI also discovered that, for people ages one to forty-six, trauma is the leading cause of death.[13]

Dr. William Worden, a leading psychologist and author of *Grief Counseling and Grief Therapy,* explains sudden deaths. He writes that sudden deaths are essentially events that occur without warning.[14] He seems to agree with Dyer but explains that the grief dynamics surrounding sudden deaths are more complex.[15] That is, they are more complex than those involving anticipated deaths, where there is some warning. As with traumatic deaths, sudden deaths are likely to shatter the worlds of those who grieve.[16]

The Centers for Disease Control and Prevention also published statistics related to cause of death by age. These recent findings revealed that the leading cause of traumatic death for people between the ages of ten and thirty-five was suicide. This same report also showed that the three major causes of death for all

---

[11] Jack Claridge. *Expore Forensics.* January 6, 2016. http://www.exporeforensics.org (accessed February 1, 2016).

[12] *National Trauma Insitute.* January 1, 2017. http://www.nationaltraumainsitute.org (accessed June 2, 2017).

The site was updated to reflect findings in 2017.

[13] Ibid.

[14] William J. Worden. *Grief Counseling and Grief Theropy: A Handbook for Practical Mental Health Practitioners.* (New York: Springer Publishing Company, 2002): 127.

[15] Ibid., 125.

[16] Ibid., 40.

ages, one to sixty-four, were unintentional deaths, homicide, and suicide.[17] These studies were conducted nationwide.

The National Violent Death Reporting System (NVDRS) tracks all deaths each year per state. Recently, NVDRS reported that there were 960 violent deaths in South Carolina alone.[18] These deaths occurred as a result of various means, including vehicles, weapons, and tools, covering all genders as well as ethnic diversities. Dyer's explanation of trauma or sudden death, then, involves all these incidents.

This information portrays the context in which this research is conducted: local congregations and communities. Going forward, these statistical findings will also address the need for pastoral care. This next section amplifies the need for pastoral care in response to traumatic events. In so doing, it lays the foundation for the need for preaching as a modality of pastoral care.

Since the geographical context concerns primarily South Carolina, it is helpful to highlight recent studies affecting South Carolinians. In 1989, Hurricane Hugo slammed into the coast of South Carolina, causing 6.5 billion dollars' worth of damage to residential as well as commercial properties. Although this event affected mainly North and South Carolina, it also affected the Eastern Seaboard of the United States.[19] Following the event, 1.8 million people were affected by the storm, with over sixty

---

[17] *Centers for Disease Control and Prevention.* January 1, 2017. https://www.cdc.gov/violenceprevention/nvdrs (accessed December 15, 2017).

[18] *National Trauma Institute.* January 1, 2017. These statistics were presented in September 2014, the twenty-fifth anniversary of Hurricane Hugo.

[19] South Carolina Emergency Management Division. January 1, 2017. http://www.scemd.org (accessed June 2, 2020.)

thousand being displaced. Thousands of those displaced residents were from South Carolina.

A study conducted among South Carolina residents a few years after the event revealed that three out of four survivors of the hurricane utilized religion as a coping strategy.[20] The results of this study also prompted some researchers to investigate this matter further. Researchers wanted to understand the validity of pastoral intervention as a major resource for the bereaved. Studies showed that in times of traumatic death, fewer people seek assistance from a mental health professional. As a matter of fact, they are five times more likely to consult clergy.[21] So, essentially, 54 percent of people experiencing a trauma of some type choose support from a pastor/rabbi/priest/imam before they will seek help from a mental health counselor.

What these results suggest is that when people experience a traumatic loss, such as traumatic death, they will more likely seek support from a minister. It must be noted, however, that these findings do not diminish the role of mental health professionals. Rather, they amplify the value of pastoral intervention for bereavement as a partner in mental health.[22] In short, these studies merely demonstrate the need for pastoral care in light of recent tragedies in South Carolina.

These findings, then, intensify the cry for pastoral involvement in times of grief resulting from trauma. Moreover, these studies

---

[20] Andrew Weaver et al. Authored "Post Traumatic Stress, Mental Health Professionals, and the Clergy: A Need for Collaboration, Training, and Research." *Journal on Traumatic Stress*, 1996: 847–856.

[21] Ibid., 847–848.

[22] Ibid., 847–848.

stand as a reminder for pastors that they cannot simply hear the cries and ignore them. Rather, pastors must bring to their congregations the gifts that God has invested in them. More importantly, though, they must bring the ministry of the Word. Correspondingly, this next section will exhibit models of pastoral care from the scriptures.

Part 1.3 Biblical Models of Pastoral Care

These preceding studies undergird the irreplaceable role of pastoral care in times of trauma. They also prove what scripture has always taught about the place for pastors in human affairs. That is, God established the role of the pastor to care for the sheep. Ephesians 4:11–13 clarifies the role of pastoring.

> "And he gave some, apostles; and some, prophets; and some, evangelists; and some, pastors and teachers; for the perfecting of the saints, for the work of the ministry, for the edifying of the body of Christ: Till we all come in the unity of the faith, and of the knowledge of the Son of God, unto a perfect man, unto the measure of the stature of the fullness of Christ."

This passage also contradicts any thought that pastoral care is a human institution. God established the role of pastors particularly in the body of Christ. Their purpose, Paul therefore explains, is for the *equipping* of the saints of God, that is, for ministry or service to the Lord.

Pastoral care can be observed in the Old Testament. In Joshua

10:25, for instance, one can hear a pastor's encouragement in the face of potential disaster. Joshua says, "And Joshua said unto them 'Fear not, nor be dismayed, be strong and of good courage: for they shall the Lord do to all your enemies against whom ye fight." This verse proclaims words of comfort and hope. As the attendant and priest for Moses, Joshua was accustomed to providing pastoral care.

Zechariah, the prophet, also exhorted a troubled people from the Word of the Lord. In Zechariah 8, he urged Israel to be strong and not to lose heart. Verses 14 through 17, then, contain the prophetic words from God that give inspiration to the prophet's words. It should also be noted that Zechariah, Jeremiah, and Ezekiel were of the priestly lineage of Berechiah. It is no wonder, then, that the heart of a pastor is reflected through Zechariah, a prophet.

New Testament passages also speak to pastoral care, giving descriptions of how it should look. In Matthew 25:35–36, Jesus teaches His disciples how to have compassion on those who cannot fend for themselves. In addition to demonstrating compassion, Jesus also taught them to speak hope in the same way. He said, "For I was an hungered, and ye gave me meat; I was thirsty and ye gave me drink: I was a stranger, and ye took me in: Naked, and ye clothed me: I was sick, and ye visited me: I was in prison and ye came unto me.."

In one instance, Jesus personally exhibited a feature of pastoral care that was in some ways controversial as well as unorthodox. In John 8:1–11, the Pharisees brought a woman caught in adultery and set her before Jesus. Tenny describes the manner in which the Pharisees brought her to Him as "forceful." The adverb *forceful* indicates she had already experienced some type of trauma at the hands of the Pharisees.[23] Rather than exhibiting harsh condemnation on the woman, Jesus demonstrated spiritual and emotional care, leading to her restoration.

Acts 20:28 portrays another biblical example of pastoral care. In Acts 20, Paul encouraged the elders of the Ephesian church to take care of themselves and their parishioners. In so doing, he urged the elders to "take heed" to the needs of their people. The word *heed* (προσέχω) means to *watch out for* or *pay close attention.*[24] Paul, therefore, employed pastoral encouragement to the Ephesian elders to exercise the same encouragement to their parishioners. He was, in fact, modeling what he taught.

One can also observe the theme of pastoral care elsewhere in the New Testament. In James 1:2–12, for example, James addresses the issue of perseverance in the face of tribulation. The Jews were experiencing persecution because of their faith in Christ and, as a result, many of them were discouraged. Accordingly, James urged them not to give up but to persevere through prayer. Although to some people this encouragement may seem trivial, James's advice was biblically sound. It was sound advice because he was exercising pastoral care and guidance to a visibly grieving people who were also experiencing a crisis. Prayer, therefore, was the path through the crisis.

The pastor's heart is also visible in James 5:7–12. Here, James exhorts his readers to "establish" their "hearts" in the Lord's

---

[23] Merril C. Tenney. *John: The Gospel of Belief: An Analytic Study of the Text.* (Grand Rapids: Eerdmans Publishing Company 1988): 14.

[24] Kurt Aland et al., *The Greek New Testament,* (Deutsche Bibelgesellshaft. Stuttgart 2006): 545.

return. In doing so, he was also encouraging them to retain their hope in the Lord in light of the increasing tribulations around them. Out of fear that some Jews might succumb to external pressures, James exercised his pastoral calling. He urged them all to hold tightly to their trust in God. These models simply present pastors with biblical precedents for pastoral care. These passages, then, demonstrate how pastoral care is actuated. The way in which pastors interpret scripture, of course, varies.

CONTEMPORARY PERSPECTIVES ON PASTORAL CARE

When discussing pastoral care, one must prepare for the complexities that abound. Scripture shows that pastoral care is the heart and soul of shepherding. In short, it is the work of the pastor. A review of contemporary perspectives on pastoral care presented certain questions.

First, what is pastoral care? It may come as a surprise that there are different perspectives. Second, what are critical elements to pastoral care making it necessary to congregational health? Context and personal needs help identify these elements. Third, what is the necessity of post trauma pastoral care? Authors have varying opinions on this matter. Finally, where does preaching fit into pastoral care? All these questions are addressed in the next five perspectives.

Part 1.4.1 The First Perspective

As pastor of Grace Community Church in Sun Valley, California, John MacArthur is a renowned author and teacher. In *Pastoral Ministry*, he defines pastoral care. His treatise on pastoral care, however, is derived from questions posed by other pastors. One of the questions asked of MacArthur was his perspective on pastoral ministry. He explains:

> Everything is built on what we understand Scripture to teach and the pattern for ministry it clearly lays out: edifying, leading people to the Lord's Table, baptizing, discipline, training, evangelizing locally, and sending to the fields of the world. All such efforts are led by the plurality of godly men and apply it to the people.[25]

MacArthur's passion about obedience to the scriptures is evident. Moreover, it is clear from his perspective that the Word of God is central to the ministry of pastoral ministry. Not only that, but pastoral ministry is impossible without obedience to the Word of God. The Word of God, in MacArthur's opinion, is therefore not only important to but also at the core of pastoral ministry.

MacArthur defended two important traits of pastoral ministry—humility and shepherding—and he drew these lessons from 1 Peter 5:2–4 where Peter writes:

---

[25] John MacArthur. *Pastoral Ministry: How to Shepherd Biblically*. (Nashville: Thomas Nelson Inc. 2005): 18.

> "Feed the flock of God which is among you, taking the oversight therefore, not by constraint, but willingly; not for filthy lucre, but of a ready mind; neither as being lords over God's heritage, but being ensamples to the flock. And when the chief Shepherd shall appear, ye shall receive a crown of glory that fadeth not away."

Commenting on 1 Peter 5, MacArthur accentuated two important points in pastoral care.

Humility is the benchmark of the true servant of God.[26] One is able to connect with the Lord and be the hands of God that bring comfort to the mourning only through a spirit of humility. Humility furthermore allows for a correct view of God in the minister's life and ministry. When one has a correct view of God in his or her spiritual life, one is then able to execute a genuine type of caring ministry.[27] Only then, MacArthur continues, is the servant able to confidently operate in God's power and be committed to His truth.[28]

Another key term in this passage is *shepherding*. Notice again how 1 Peter 5:1-4 approaches the ministry of *shepherding*. He uses shepherding to characterize the manner in which pastors execute their pastoral duties.

> "The elders which are among you I exhort, who am also an elder, and a witness of the sufferings of Christ, and also a partaker of the glory that shall be

---

[26] Ibid., 18.

[27] Ibid., 22.

[28] Ibid., 23.

revealed: feed the flock of God which is among you, taking the oversight therefore, not by constraint, but willingly; not for filthy lucre, but of a ready mind; neither as being lords over God's heritage, but being ensamples to the flock. And when the chief Shepherd shall appear, ye shall receive a crown of glory that fadeth not away."

MacArthur responds to this passage by explaining that it unequivocally demonstrates the integrity and true function of shepherds in the local church. He also argues that it implies a style of leadership in which people are valued rather than utilized.[29]

Further study into the role of the shepherding in the church reveals certain leadership responsibilities. The first responsibility is leadership through example. As Peter explains, pastors lead by emulating the very principles they teach.[30] The second responsibility is leading by administration. In leading by administration, the pastor places emphasis on meeting the physical needs of congregants.[31] Leading by example and administration are clearly critical in shepherding.

Two additional responsibilities further elucidate the role of shepherding. MacArthur next accentuates the nurturing of the flock. Nurturing the flock not only applies to spiritual development but also embodies the process of intervention in times of trauma.

---

[29] MacArthur explained how humility and servitude were at the heart of the pastoral leadership versus secular leadership, which often centers on power over people (MacArthur, *Pastoral Ministry*, 23).

[30] This is an example of exemplified leadership (MacArthur, *Pastoral Ministry*, 23).

[31] Leading by administration as applied by MacArthur is more concerned with member care than administrative (MacArthur, *Pastoral Ministry*, 23).

Then, there is cultivating maturity. When cultivating maturity, pastors lead their parishioners into scriptural principles.[32] These scriptural principles equip people who are facing the realities of life such as pain and suffering.

According to MacArthur, an important area of pastoral leadership involves guarding one's flock from potential harm. In fact, he demonstrates that one of the ways in which pastors guard congregations from harm is dedicating themselves to defending the Word.[33] In defending the Word, the pastors preach biblically sound doctrine and guard God's flock from the harms of potential heresies through biblical preaching. The emphasis here is on preaching the Word of God properly. All these responsibilities of leadership directly impact the pastor's ministry of support for a congregation during difficult times.

MacArthur discusses an avenue through which these responsibilities are expressed. He contends that this primary avenue is preaching.[34] MacArthur furthermore describes a benefit of preaching in the process of conveying these responsibilities. He also points out that preaching communicates emotional care in times of traumatic loss. The point is that preaching is a means of connecting with a traumatized congregation. Therefore, pastors miss this important connection when they fail to emphasize the emotional aspect.

Spiritual cultivation also has an indispensable place in

---

[32] Ibid., 23.

[33] The task of defending the flock of God is also one that God had entrusted to His undershepherds (MacArthur, *Pastoral Ministry,* 23).

[34] In keeping with MacArthur's main focus, which is preaching, the manner in which he approaches pulpit ministry is absolutely critical to pastoral care. Ibid., 24.

preaching.[35] Pastors, according to MacArthur, have responsibilities to not only defend against doctrinal heresy but also contribute to the emotional and spiritual growth of parishioners. That said the exposition of scripture is key to one's emotional and spiritual growth. This insight, therefore, demonstrates a connection between spiritual cultivation and emotional maturity. Pastors must also preach to cultivate the faith of saints to deal effectively with sadness and loss.

Part 1.4.2 A Second Perspective

Victor Lehman proffers a second perspective on pastoral care in *The Work of the Pastor*. His emphasis throughout his development of pastoral care is on shepherding. Lehman, however, describes a less attractive side. Using the imagery of the "shepherd as the door to the sheep fold," he portrays Jesus's pastoral care in a sacrificial manner.[36] This striking imagery of the shepherd not only places him at the fold's entrance, but also positions him as the sheep's protector. Whoever or whatever, then, seeks to harm the sheep is forced to face the shepherd.[37] Jesus's imagery certainly presents a less glamorous side to ministry than people realize.

Lehman's example draws from Jesus's self-description of Himself as the Shepherd who lays down His life for His sheep. In John 10:11 Jesus explains His purpose by saying, "I am the good

---

[35] Notice the close relationship that MacArthur draws between pastoral work and preaching.

[36] Victor D. Lehman. *The Work of the Pastor.* (Valley Forge: Judson Press, 2004): 184. Lehman presented a brief chapter on the work of the pastor, accentuating various highlights of pastoral ministry.

[37] Ibid., 34.

Shepherd. The good Shepherd lays down His life for the sheep."
Lehman accordingly explains that pastors are similarly called to
sacrifice themselves for the lives of their sheep.[38] The manner
in which they are to lay down their lives is through sacrificing
themselves as they dedicate their entire lives to the betterment of
those they serve.

Part 1.4.3 A Third Perspective

Derek Prime and Allister Begg together compose a third perspective
on pastoral care in their work entitled *On Being a Pastor.* Their
approach emphasizes shepherding as a defining imagery for the
pastoral role. From MacArthur's perspective, shepherding focuses
on *feeding* the sheep, which primarily emphasizes the Word.
Lehman, interestingly, accentuates Jesus as the door to the fold.

Prime and Begg, however, produce a broader view of pastoral
care through developing additional key areas. These areas are
preaching, congregational support, bereavement ministry, and
visitation. Although some of their work seems repetitive, the
depth at which they formulate their positions is impressive and
informative.

From the outset, Prime and Begg unequivocally establish a
definition of the pastoral calling. The pastor's purpose, they state,
is to be a shepherd.[39] As the shepherd, the pastor is charged by God

---

[38] Using Jesus's life as an example, Lehman accentuates the call to pastors to
commit themselves to the proper care for their congregations (Lehman, *Work of
the Pastor,* 34–35).

[39] Derek Begg and Alister Prime. *On Being a Pastor: Understanding Our Calling and
Work.* (Chicago: Moody Publishers, 2004): 149–150. Their discussion of pastoral
ministry focuses on pastoral care as it applies mainly to the local parish.

to serve in the same spirit as did Jesus. That is to say, the pastor is a servant. The temptation to fulfill pastoral duties in any other role than as the servant-leader is a grave mistake. Seeking to fulfill pastoral duties as anything less than a servant is essentially selfish. Pastors, accordingly, must always remember their roles as God's undershepherds.[40]

In Matthew 20: 20-21, for example, James's and John's mother approaches Jesus. Her purpose is to secure a place of honor for her children in Jesus's kingdom. Even though He understood her true intentions, Jesus did not reprimand her. Rather, He used her question to impart a profound lesson to all who follow Him. He responded in verses 27-28, "And whomever will be chief among you, let him be your servant; even as the Son of Man came not to be ministered unto, but to minister and to give his life a ransom for many." This scenario, therefore, begs the question: what is the basis for being a pastor, a minister or a shepherd? It is to be a servant.

Shepherding is synonymous with pastoral work.[41] Albeit this description may sound simplistic, it is nonetheless a true characterization. Shepherding, as Begg and Prime continued, is more than a practice or a routine. It is an attitude central to the pastor's heart. In shepherding, the pastor commits his life to the care and welfare of the congregation. Pastors should therefore emulate Jesus as He cares for His flock.

In developing their perspective of pastoral care, Begg and Prime describe two key elements. One of these elements is knowledge

---

[40] Ibid., 150.

[41] At this point, it is clear that a running theme through research is shepherding as an imagery of pastoral work.

of one's sheep.[42] This element is of course realized when there is a personal connection between the pastor and the congregation. How else will a pastor truly know who is hurting or frightened or insecure? Pastors most effectively know their congregations when they visit regularly. In visitation, furthermore, pastors are better able to not only identify but also assess people's needs.

Another essential element to pastoral work is love. Although this point should go without saying, it seems that love has often become disassociated during routine business. In *On Being a Pastor,* the authors contended that pastors can implement a practical expression of love—by giving time. This is both a practical and most appreciated expression of love. Prime and Begg contend:

> If we love people we will give them our time—
> and that includes our families who must never
> be neglected because of our care for others. The
> stewardship of time in pastoral ministry is a
> constant battle. There are obvious limits to the
> time that we have available, especially if it is in the
> morning when we properly give priority to study
> and preparation or ministry. But there are occasions
> each week when we can make ourselves available
> to people and although they may not seem at first
> sight particularly significant, we believe they are.[43]

---

[42] While the Good Shepherd already knows His sheep, undershepherds do not. It is therefore incumbent upon undershepherds to establish a personal knowledge base in order to effectively fulfill their callings (Begg and Prime, *On Being a Pastor,* 151).

[43] The authors identified time as one the greatest gifts of pastoral ministry (Begg and Prime, *On Being a Pastor,* 151).

In the course of developing their understanding of pastoral work, Prime and Begg identify four definitive terms. These four words in their opinions characterize pastoral ministry.[44] The first two terms are *encouragement* and *exhortation*. Encouragement is the activity of the pastor coming alongside parishioners to undergird their lives. Another important theme for pastoral ministry is exhortation.[45] Exhortation, they explain, is the virtue that points people in the direction of the Lord. In *Christian Counseling*, Gary Collins likewise defines exhortation as "coming alongside to help."[46]

Two other important terms are *admonition* and *counseling*. Admonition, to start with, is similar to encouragement and counseling, yet distinct. As with encouragement and exhortation, admonition speaks to the pastor's intentional involvement in the parishioner's life. Admonition, however, differs from encouragement and counseling as it is manifested in various contexts. Even if counseling and encouragement are usually need-based interventions, one exercises admonition through preaching, teaching, and dialogue.

The next term, *counseling*, is essential to the pastoral ministry of counseling. Although counseling sounds as though the minister assumes the role of a psychologist, this notion is not quite the case. Pastoral counseling entails conversations with a parishioner that lead to understanding personal needs in light of certain spiritual

---

[44] Without oversimplifying the pastoral ministry, the authors sought to isolate main themes that characterize pastoral care (Begg and Prime, *On Being a Pastor*, 164).

[45] Ibid., 164.

[46] Gary R. Collins. *Christian Counseling*. (Dallas: Word Publishing, 1988): 26. Collins interestingly does not give much credence to visitation.

dynamics. These spiritual dynamics include the ministry of the Holy Spirit through the Word of God to the grieving child of God.[47] Moreover, pastoral counseling is also many times a faith-based ministry.

A review of *Ministry of the* Pastor at this point raises a question pertinent to the research process. What relationship do these terms have with preaching? The authors, in fact, see a direct correlation between these terms and preaching. That correlation, they argue, culminates into one thought. That thought is the power of the healing balm of the Word of God. Preachers enable healing processes in grieving parishioners when they accentuate the healing balm of the Word of God. This healing process, therefore, is where pastoral care and preaching intersect. Begg and Prime responded to this intersection by declaring:

> A great benefit of being a pastor of those whom we teach is that we are able to apply the Word to the known needs of the people under our care. We do not mean by this that when we discern a need, we immediately frame a sermon to meet it. But as we get to know people well, visiting them in their crises and serving them in various circumstances, our application of God's Word will be consciously and helpfully by our assimilation of their experiences and cries for direction.[48]

---

[47] In terms of counseling, the author focused on spiritual dynamics while giving proper attention to emotional and psychological dynamics as well (Collins, *Christian Counseling*, 129).

[48] Ibid., 129.

Part 1.4.4 A Fourth Perspective

In the first perspective, MacArthur examines the importance of feeding the sheep in pastoral care. Then, Lehman highlights the self-sacrificial element of shepherding. From there, Begg and Prime accentuate the important elements of pastoral care. With those elements in mind, the authors note that these elements characterize pastoral ministry and preaching. Next, we see a fourth perspective.

John W. Frye, in his book *Jesus the Pastor,* presented a moving discussion. Underscoring Jesus's caring and nurturing mannerisms, Frye exalted the Lord as the epitome of pastoral care. His proposition is that pastoral care's main purpose is to "to bring people to God."[49] Frye further explained that Jesus fulfilled this purpose though His pastoral care. In so doing, Frye also demonstrated how Jesus was the supreme example for all pastors. He wrote:

> This concept is not new. It is, however, sadly missing from many discussions on pastoral ministry. Grounded firmly in the bedrock of scriptural revelation is the Chief Shepherd. Our common word *pastor* has made its way to us through Latin and is simply the semantic equivalent of the biblical word for *shepherd.* It is the title that Jesus wore gladly and redeemed by His life and ministry. The term *pastor (shepherd)* may be gutted of value in our

---

[49] John W. Frye. *Jesus as Pastor.* (Grand Rapids: Zondervan Publishing House, 2000): 147–148.

culture (even in our evangelical culture), but is never downplayed by Jesus or the New Testament writers. Jesus Christ is the supreme shepherd and thus the ultimate senior pastor.[50]

Frye's argument is that if one wants to learn how to be a pastor, one must look at Jesus's example. Obviously, who would contend with that point of view? Still, as the writer emphasizes, this perspective is missing from many lectures on pastoral ministry. Scripture nonetheless gives clear examples where Jesus as the chief shepherd exhibits Himself as the great pastor.[51]

A famous passage that exemplifies Jesus as the chief shepherd is John 4. This chapter portrays Jesus doing something highly unorthodox. It depicts Him approaching a Samaritan woman at Jacob's well. No other Jewish male, not to mention religious leader, would have considered breaching such a cultural barrier. Jesus, however, breached that barrier. He proceeded to assess her deeper needs and minister as a shepherd. He then defended the woman from those who sought to devour her publically. Instead of upbraiding the woman and further humiliating her, Jesus demonstrated love and forgiveness as the path to God.[52]

Note how in verse 7 Jesus enters the conversation. He says to her, "Give Me a drink." At this point, the woman is astounded that a Jewish male has spoken with her. From that moment, a conversation erupts that almost immediately becomes personal.

---

[50] Ibid., 48.

[51] Frye illustrated from Jesus's life an unrelenting faithfulness to God's call (*Jesus as Pastor*, 148).

[52] See *Jesus as Pastor*, 48, where Frye accentuates Jesus's courageous pastoral ministry.

Jesus is purposefully presenting the gift of life through the offering of Himself.

Eventually, the conversation highlights her current social life. When asked about her husband, the woman replies she has none—which Jesus applauds. All the while, though, he is not judgmental. Jesus listens with compassion while exhibiting exhortation and admonition. His purpose, it would appear, is not to browbeat her into confession, but to restore her.

What, then, are some observations for pastors? To start with, Frye explains that people are fallen, fragile vessels and as such struggle with issues. He then declares that pastors most effectively engage these issues through pastoral visits.[53] Though these issues should not dominate the conversations, they should still be addressed. The lesson is that the person is the point of pastoral care, not just the issues.

Another important observation was that Jesus was a *people-grounded person*.[54] In describing Jesus as a people person, Frye meant that Jesus was about nurturing people. This description of Jesus does not diminish His commitment to the Father's plan for His life. Rather, it implies that Jesus sought always to be in touch with His creation. He loved people and so wanted to be near them and with them.

A final observation gleaned from John 4 was His ability to teach. Teaching was paramount to the ministry of Jesus. In

---

[53] Frye makes it clear that pastoral visits, though, must have some substantive ministry component to them (Frye, *Jesus as Pastor,* 48).

[54] Jesus mastered the abilities of being people focused while maintaining unwavering mindfulness of His role in God's kingdom on earth (Frye, *Jesus as Pastor,* 48–49).

teaching moments, Jesus's purpose was not necessarily to impart information or to indoctrinate. Rather, His aim was to change lives and draw people's hearts to God.[55] In fact, He accomplished this feat through being the Word of Life.

Likewise, teaching must also be paramount to the ministry of pastors. Since Jesus was and is the Word of Life, pastors must therefore preach the Word of Life. With this declaration in mind, Frye argues that when pastors preach the Word of Life, they in fact proclaim the hope of humanity. No other means exists by which people may know hope other than through the Word. Consequently, pastors are obedient to their call as shepherds when they preach the Word of Life.

Part 1.4.5 A Fifth Perspective

Arthur Teikmanis advocates a fifth perspective in *Pastoral Care and Preaching*. He portrays pastoral care as an evangelistic as well as a nurturing activity. In his estimation, the pastor's purpose is to reach people with the grace and hope of Christ. Similar to Frye's perspective, Teikmanis also looks at how Jesus pastored people. Although the pastor serves as the undershepherd for a local congregation, the minister is nonetheless somewhat of a missionary.[56]

In fact, the author contends that evangelism is "sine qua non"

---

[55] Ibid., 48.

[56] Teikmanis, Arthur L., *Preaching and Pastoral Care.*(Philadelphia: Fortess Press, 1964): 48. Although dated, Teikmainis's was one of few sources that spoke directly to pastoral preaching. He described pastors as shepherds and missionaries.

of discipleship, meaning an essential quality.[57] Pastors, therefore, should always be about the business of leading people to God. This contention is akin to Frye's proposition about pastoral ministry as bringing people to God. As previously mentioned, Teikmanis envisions an even deeper purpose for pastors. Pastors serve to not only "save their souls" but also comfort their heavy hearts.

The author discusses visiting as one of the essential tasks to comforting the heavy-hearted. He prefers to describe pastoral visits as "calling."[58] He furthermore explains that pastoral calling is central to effective pastoral care. Pastors most effectively learn more about their people through calling. In pastoral calling, pastors are in a place where they in fact comfort the heavy laden. It is therefore necessary for pastors to be approachable, compassionate, nonjudgmental, insightful, and ready to lead people to God.

Furthermore, pastors preach more effectively when they engage their parishioners individually.[59] Teikmanis explains, "I submit this volume not as a startling discovery, but as a testimony that preaching and pastoral care are dynamically and inseparably bound together. In many ways, preaching lives on in pastoral ministry." Pastoral ministry, when faithfully conducted through pastoral care, undergirds pastoral preaching.

---

[57] As a central theme to his book, Teikmanis weighed heavily on preaching as an essential aspect to pastoral work.

[58] Ibid., 28.

[59] By this thought, Teikmanis meant that preachers should preach with the needs of the parishioners in mind (Teikmanis, *Preaching and Pastoral Care,* 28).

PASTORAL PREACHING

Teikmanis's comments on preaching and pastoral care, therefore, segue into the next section, "Pastoral Preaching." There are two parts to this section. The first part develops a conceptualization through discussing various points of view. The second part focuses on the ministry of the Word in pastoral preaching. In the second part, research also seeks to demonstrate how to employ the Word in pastoral preaching.

Part 2.1 Conceptualizing Pastoral Preaching

The literature review revealed that most scholars believed there was a relationship between pastoral care and preaching. However, these same scholars tended to differ in terms of the proximity in relationship between preaching and pastoral care. Research then examined divergent points of view regarding this proximity and revealed that most scholars affirmed that preaching was at least important to pastoral care if not most important. This next section, then, examines preaching as a modality of pastoral care.

Part 2.1.1 First Concept of Pastoral Preaching

In their book, *Preaching God's Compassion*, Leroy Aden and Robert Hughes argued for compassion as an essential element to preaching.[60] This essential element of compassion and its relationship with preaching was the basic premise for their book. The ministry

---

[60] Leroy H. Aden and Robert G. Hughes. *Preaching God's Compassion.* (Minneapolis: Augsburg Fortress Press, 2002): 64. The authors acknowledge the daunting task of preaching God's compassion and the divine mandate to do so (Aden and Hughes, *Preaching God's Compassion,* 81).

of compassion, they explained, is also most effectively conveyed when the preacher expounds on the Word of God. Expounding the scriptures essentially gives God's compassion an audible voice, making preaching pastoral in nature. The writers accordingly defined pastoral preaching as "the oral proclamation of God's Word from the perspective of caring for or comforting people in need."[61]

Next, the authors describe two types of pastoral preaching often employed. The first type is direct communication, which is appropriate when it is necessary to speak plainly about an issue. For instance, in direct preaching, the minister may confront a false doctrine concerning suffering and sin. In contrast, indirect communication occurs when the speaker discusses the parameters of an issue without voicing the issue plainly. In review of these definitions, the authors contend that indirect communication should be employed when speaking compassion.[62]

To substantiate their positions from biblical literature, the authors cited examples of Jesus's teaching ministry. Jesus, they noted, often employed indirect communication when comforting the bereaved.[63] Additionally, Jesus also employed indirect communication to breach the virtual impervious shells of unbelief in His listeners. As one example, Luke 16:19–23 says:

> "There was a certain rich man who was clothed in purple and fine linen and fared sumptuously every day. But there was a certain beggar named Lazarus,

---

[61] Ibid., ix.

[62] Ibid., 81.

[63] Ibid., 82.

which was laid at his gate, full of sores, and desiring to be fed with the crumbs which fell from the rich man's table: moreover the dogs came and licked his sores. And it came to pass, that the beggar died, and was carried by the angels into Abraham's bosom: the rich man also died and was buried. And in Hell, he lifted up his eyes being in torments, seeth Abraham afar off, and Lazarus in his bosom."

Examples such as the preceding one illustrate an important point. The hearers of Jesus's parables were rarely the subjects of said parables. As a result, those listening to Jesus rarely felt that their personal business was being exposed in public. Whether comforting the bereaved or imparting a spiritual lesson, Jesus respected people, according to the writers.

Jesus also employed direct communication. In such instances, Jesus typically spoke directly to people in an effort to refute false conceptions. For instance, in Matthew 5: 43-46, Jesus virtually dismantles the teachings of the Pharisees' concept of love as He argues:

"Ye have heard that it hath been said, 'Thou shalt love thy neighbour and hate thine enemy.' But I say unto you, love your enemies, bless them that curse you, do good to them that hate you, and pray for them which despitefully use you and persecute you; that ye may be the children of your Father which is in heaven: for He maketh His sun rise on the evil and on the good, and sendeth rain on the just and on the unjust. For if ye love them which love you, what reward have ye? do not even the publicans do the same?"

These methods, the writers argue, are effective when addressing issues affecting an entire congregation. Situations exist when the proverbial elephant in the room must be named directly. A couple of examples of these "elephants" are either suicide or homicide. Conversely, it is appropriate at times for the issue to remain anonymous. In such times, speaking indirectly enables the gospel truth to be heard without causing offense.

People often have different perspectives on grief. When preparing to preach, therefore, the authors warn against "magical" thinking. In magical thinking, they explain that the preacher intimates that the Lord will always remove the pain.[64] This type of preaching not only misrepresents scripture but also imposes guilt upon the sufferer when the pain does not diminish. Notwithstanding good intentions, preachers may form weak foundations of faith.

When addressing grief, the writers say that preachers should speak in a way that acknowledges the grief. Moreover, as opposed to preaching around the grief, the authors encourage ministers to identify the grief.[65] Scripture demonstrates how Christ suffered on various levels. Demonstrating Christ's sufferings from scripture,

---

[64] The writers warn against a type of thinking among many preachers called "magical thinking" that compels preachers to mishandle grief from the pulpit (Aden and Hughes, *Preaching and Compassion,* 16–17).

[65] Ibid.

then, conveys how He identifies with His children in all aspects of their grief.

In light of this, Aden and Hughes urge preachers to proceed with a cross-centered theology, which focuses on the suffering element of Jesus's sacrifice. Focusing on Jesus's suffering at the cross allows mourners the freedom to grieve. A cross-centered theology also reminds mourners that sin is not the cause of all suffering.[66]

Next, the authors present three considerations regarding goals for pastoral preaching. First, pastoral preaching should give voice to the lament. Giving voice to lament may assist a grieving congregation, for example, in acknowledging their feelings. Second, pastoral preaching should assist the bereaved to face the reality that they are redeemed through Christ. Third, pastoral preaching should speak hope into the grieving hearts of the sufferers. This hope, the authors noted, is to be found in the abiding love of God through Christ.[67]

In overview, the ideas proposed by Aden and Hughes have both strengths and weaknesses. Regarding direct and indirect speaking, the authors did well in explaining the benefits of these modes. The authors failed to mention, however, exactly how these ideas could be applied. It is also helpful to have an explanation on how these principles are communicated to congregations. Nonetheless, the ideas do have some inherent value to them.

The writers also presented an excellent concept in cross-centered theology. Preaching from the cross nullifies certain

---

[66] Cross-centered preaching emphasizes the sufferings of Christ (Aden and Hughes, *Preaching and Compassion*, 21–22).

[67] These goals suggest directions in preaching to a grieving congregation.

misconceptions, such as suffering derives only from sin. The writers, though, did not expound widely on Jesus's life. Finally, the goals for a pastoral sermon were practical and prudent as presented. Solid objectives enforce effective preaching.

Part 2.1.2 The Second Concept of Pastoral Preaching

Aden and Hughes presented an approach grounded in a Christ-centered theology with emphasis on speaking to pain. In *Spirit Speech,* Luke Powery contends for pastoral preaching from a cultural perspective. As an ordained minister in the African Methodist Episcopal Church, Powery speaks from a heritage that has historically conjoined two homiletic themes: lament and celebration. In celebration, the writer explains, the preacher celebrates the wonder of hope as a divine gift.[68] That hope rests on the promise of an eternal reunion with one's long-deceased friends and relatives. This hope, the author asserted, is the basis for celebration in preaching.

Conversely, there is the theme of lament in preaching. The element of lament, Powery described, gives a voice to the mourner's grief. It also allows listeners to hear the reality and presence of pain in the gospels. The blessing from lament is found in its honesty before God.[69] Honesty in lament happens when the preacher gives voice to suffering in sermons instead of circumventing the issue.

Powery writes that preachers often see lament and celebration as counter thematic, implying that celebration and lament

---

[68] Luke A. Powery. *Spirit Speech.* (Nashville: Abingdon Press, 2009): 16–17. Powery speaks from his own faith tradition.

[69] Expressing lament from the pulpit is actually a means of giving people the freedom to grieve without feeling guilty (Powery, *Spirit Speech,* 16–17).

are opposing themes. The truth of the matter is that there is collaboration between the two in that they are homiletic themes that actually add an element of holism to a sermon. Preaching lament mixed with celebration also allows the believer hear the truth in both.

Likewise, Powery explains that celebration is the place where the sufferer engages as a worshipper while still lamenting. He believes this point is important since some preachers do not believe that lament and celebration can coexist in worship. Through celebration, the individual is able to experience God's grace that is sufficient for all of humanity's ailments[70] and to know the presence of God in the midst of lament. All the while, the mourner accesses the peace of God. Lamenting the pain while celebrating God's grace, then, is a sacred and rich place for the mourner.

Going deeper, Powery declared that *homiletical lament* is a sermonic form that declares and acknowledges the suffering of congregants.[71] Although mentioning one's suffering is important to homiletical lament, it is not the sermon's core. Rather, preaching lament continues with an emphasis upon the grace and presence of God.

Ministers often fear that preaching lament is too emotional. This fear also causes many ministers to overlook the emotional element in scripture. In reality, Powery says, preaching lament names the suffering that people are dealing with at the moment.

---

[70] In preaching, Powery interposes two opposing themes in a way that they complement each other rather than compete (Powery, *Spirit Speech,* 92).

[71] Homiletical lament, Powery explained, begins with lamenting pain and then moves toward hope (Powery, *Spirit Speech,* 92).

As a result, three important elements bring strength and relevancy to the message.

To begin with, identify the reality of human pain. Preaching lament proclaims that pain is real as opposed to a figment of one's imagination. Then, employ the element of direct language. In direct language, the preacher employs imperative terminology that names the pain directly. Finally, there is the inclusion of self, which involves integrating one's personal experiences with suffering. These elements, Powery concludes, enables connection between the preacher and parishioner.[72]

Lament is important to pastoral preaching for congregations experiencing trauma. Then again, celebration is equally important to pastoral preaching.[73] Regarding celebration, there are several marks that define the celebratory sermon. The first important mark is the amplification of God's action through Christ in the world. Second, it is important to accentuate the names of God and Christ. Third, it is necessary to emphasize the concept of hope. Fourth, the preacher encourages his congregation to continue serving Christ. Finally, the preacher integrates his personal testimonies. These identifying marks, the author contends, form the basis for a celebratory sermon.

In overview of Powery's book, he certainly presented a thought-provoking approach to preaching. His primary purpose was to demonstrate how lament and celebration are essential to preaching. Throughout his book, Powery repeatedly argued that it is necessary for the preacher to simultaneously give voice

---

[72] Ibid., 98.

[73] The author reminds his readers that Christ is the good news and the reason for celebratory preaching (Powery, *Spirit Speech,* 98).

to unspoken pain while encouraging parishioners to celebrate Christ's peace.

Notwithstanding, there are some concerns. The first concern was the manner in which these elements are crafted into the sermon. The writer did not clearly explain how the preacher weaves these ideas into a particular situation. Furthermore, the writer failed to identify places in the Bible where celebration and lament are expressed sermonically. Finally, the author did not include contemporary examples of situations where lament and celebration are conveyed. Addressing these concerns would add strength to Powery's development of pastoral preaching.

Part 2.1.3 The Third Concept of Pastoral Preaching

Aden and Hughes began this section with an emphasis on the suffering of Christ. Powery then continued with a perspective that conjoined two themes, celebration and lament. This next section studies a perspective presented by J. Randall Nichols in *The Restoring Word: Preaching as Pastoral Communication*. Nichols, a seasoned psychotherapist, also brings a noteworthy perspective that stems from his long-standing career. He designs an integrative approach combining his psychotherapy with pastoral ministry. Preaching, in Nichols's estimation, is an interplay of counseling based upon biblical truths. He contends for a homiletic approach that brings both disciplines together. He calls his approach *pastoral communication*.[74]

This author begins his discussion on pastoral communication

---

[74] Randal J. Nichols. *The Restoring Word: Preaching as Pastoral Care.* (San Francisco: Harper & and Row Publishers Inc., 1987): 14–15.

with a question and follows with an explanation. Nichols wonders, "When is preaching pastoral?" He then declares:

> Isn't all preaching pastoral in one sense or another? Perhaps in a broad sense though I do not believe stopping there takes us far enough down the road of understanding what we mean. True enough, most is done by people whom the hearers identify as their pastors, and there are bound to be some connections and resonances even in the most unrelentingly theological discourse or biblical exposition. It is also true enough that all preaching is pastoral if we believe that sound theological thinking and accurate biblical understanding are in service to better personal faith, life and action.[75]

It is surmised from the author's explanation of pastoral communication that all preaching is pastoral. Nichols qualifies his position by explaining that preaching is also pastoral when it contains "sound theological thinking and accurate biblical understanding."[76]

Elaborating further, the writer contends that pastoral communication is distinguished by certain characteristics. First, preaching is considered pastoral when it has a *pastoral effect* upon its hearers. A "pastoral effect" is achieved when the sermon proclaims repentance, restoration, or encouragement. Nichols also argues

---

[75] This excerpt demonstrates how preaching is pastoral from the author's opinion (Nichols, *The Restoring Word,* 15).

[76] Ibid., 18.

that a sermon is pastoral in nature because the minister brings a message from God.

A second characteristic is a *pastoral strategy*.[77] One achieves a pastoral strategy when the sermon targets people's concerns. It is also important to note that the pastoral strategy in a sermon is achieved as biblical truths are applied to personal struggles. As Nichols explains, these approaches in a sermon enable listeners to hear their struggles being echoed in scripture. Hearing their struggles echoed in scripture strengthens the sermon with a pastoral strategy.

In the third characteristic, the author explains that communication is pastoral when it bears a *pastoral subject*.[78] The pastoral subject appeals to deeper personal need. Depression, traumatic experiences, or divorce qualify as pastoral subjects that people face in life.

The author further refines his definition by delineating two types of communication. The first type of communication is known as *prophetic* or *proclamatory* preaching.[79] In prophetic preaching, emphasis is given to the mission of the Church. In addition, prophetic preaching gives attention to the believer's personal responsibility to holiness. Second, there is *priestly* preaching. Priestly preaching emphasizes the personal needs of the parishioners. It also seeks to engage the individual parishioner where he or she is in terms of human brokenness.

---

[77] The writer explains the dominant strategy as one of the perspectives of the sermon (Nichols, *The Restoring Word*, 18).

[78] Ibid., 17–19.

[79] The author notes that the biblical-theological language of repentance, worship, faithfulness, and servanthood are typical expressions of *Prophetic Preaching*, 59.

Defining these two types of pastoral communication, the writer also explained common elements in each. The first of these common elements is *language*. Prophetic language, for instance, includes repentance, worship and individual responsibility. Priestly language alternatively emphasizes human emotions, experiences, and needs. Each of these language types has a significant place in preaching. It is accordingly incumbent upon the preacher to ensure that the pastoral subject is projected with the appropriate language.

Another element is the *direction of the message*.[80] While prophetic sermons focus on moral/ethical changes in behavior, priestly sermons conversely focus on human frailty. At times, the direction of the message contains both types of emphases.

Finally, the *nature of addressee* element is discussed. This element refers specifically to the audience. When speaking of audience, this element implies that the preacher accentuates the entire body of Christ. Rather than speaking only to a particular individual or family, the preacher speaks to the whole congregation.

These elements establish the author's definition of pastoral preaching.[81] The author then proceeds to elucidate a purpose for pastoral preaching. In fact, Nichols identifies two purposes. First, pastoral preaching seeks to enable people in discovering the love and grace of God. Second, pastoral preaching seeks to aid people in dealing realistically with their suffering.

These inherent purposes in pastoral preaching enable people to face inevitable pain. Nichols asserts that western cultures tend

---

[80] Ibid., 59.

[81] These identifying marks together form the author's perspective on how pastoral preaching is understood (Nichols, *The Restoring Word*, 59).

57

to shield people as much as possible from pain. As a result, this shielding complicates people's abilities to cope with grief. Pastoral preaching, however, responds effectively by strengthening people's abilities to cope with grief.

Preaching should also have a central focus for it to be truly pastoral. That focus, Nichols contends, is clarified when it centers on the risen Christ.[82] Preaching the risen Christ points the suffering parishioner to messages of the cross. Those messages are the reality and victory over death and, in turn, spawn hope for the future and victory over death in Christ.

Even with a clear focus, pastoral preaching is still incomplete and requires equally clear objectives in order to make it more complete.[83] First, preaching must assist people in facing the realities of grief and peace through scripture. Second, preaching must also assist people in connecting with others who share their grief. Finally, preaching must seek to empower mourners to express their emotions and own them. Overall, Nichols's approach to pastoral preaching brings the research deeper. He clearly delineates variations in pastoral communication such as priestly and prophetic preaching. Nichols also identifies qualities of each variation, though there are some areas of concern.

For example, the writer's focus was more on how the preacher can connect with grieving people—which is important—but did not clarify how scripture connects with people on the same levels. It would have been helpful to understand how a textual or an expositional preaching style speaks to trauma.

---

[82] Ibid., 41.

[83] Nichols argues that preachers should have objectives that deal with grief (Nichols, *The Restoring Word,* 41).

Part 2.1.4 A Fourth Concept of Pastoral Preaching

The first two perspectives of pastoral preaching emphasize themes drawn from scripture. Aden and Hughes developed an approach based upon the sufferings of Christ, while Powery builds his approach on lament and celebration. Both of these approaches were framed around scriptural themes in the Bible. Nichols then proposed a philosophy he calls *pastoral communication,* based on the psychotherapy and pastoral care model. His philosophy is similar in nature to the methodology in the next section.

This next section explores Edmund Holt Linn's construct for preaching in *Preaching as Counseling.* He explains his theory as a means of counseling through the art of preaching, which he says is not only a methodology but also a philosophy. Therefore, Linn insists that ministering to grieving individuals requires a different method other than preaching.[84]

Linn argues that there are two major styles of preaching, and both are ineffective. Expositional preaching is one of these styles, and he argues that it is inept at speaking to the realities of human experiences. Merely preaching from Bible stories, he further contends, does not speak adequately to people's deeper needs. Topical preaching, another style Linn deems ineffective, is where the minister builds a message from isolated passages. Linn asserts it does little in speaking to human needs. In fact, Linn points out that all these preaching styles fall short in meeting people's needs.

If these preaching styles are ineffectual, what else is there?

---

[84] Edmond Linn Holt. *Preaching as Counseling.* (Valley Forge, PA: The Judson Press, 1966): 8–10. The author relied heavily on Henry Fosdick's preaching theories.

This query fueled Linn's investigation into a style that meets human needs. At the same time, though, he was concerned about faithfulness to the Bible. He consequently sought a style that bridges these two necessities in ministry. Linn labeled his method "preaching as counseling."

At its core, the method of preaching as counseling seeks to speak pastorally to people's needs. By speaking pastorally, Linn means highlighting scriptural themes and stories that are germane to the struggles people experience.[85] It furthermore capitalizes on the emotional and psychological turmoil associated with loss. Preaching as counseling, in Linn's opinion, is therefore more effective because it begins with the basic human need.

This methodology segues into the discussion on what Linn considers essential aspects of pastoral preaching, one of which is preaching with conviction. Preaching with conviction, he declares, is necessary to the sermon's inherent forcefulness and relevancy. Conviction, however, is no replacement for proclaiming the truth of the gospel. Conviction amplifies the truth through preaching.

Another essential aspect is individual focused preaching. In individual focused preaching, the preacher speaks to the congregation as if speaking to one person and, in so doing, connects with the listener.[86] This connection, Linn then argues, allows preachers to maintain a presence of mind concerning individuals who are hurting, which he asserts is necessary. This

---

[85] Ibid., 11–12.

[86] In speaking as to one person, the writer advocated an approach wherein the preacher addresses the entire congregation as if they all feel the same general grief (Holt, *Preaching as Counseling,* 17).

type of preaching essentially reassures the listener that he or she is not alone in the suffering.

Linn also highlights other aspects in addition to preaching with conviction and establishing a connection; he also urges preachers to apply the gospel.[87] In applying the gospel, preachers demonstrate how the gospel speaks to the heart of the trauma or crisis. People in crises, says Linn, need a message from God, and applying the gospel brings a word of comfort and assurance to grieving people.

Reviewing *Preaching as Counseling,* Linn's conceptualizations presented concepts worth noting. His homiletic approach, for instance, demonstrates an essential piece to pastoral preaching, which is acknowledgment of pain. As the author explained, current preaching styles often do not give ample acknowledgment to pain. Again, it depends on the preacher as to whether or not these styles accurately acknowledge pain.

At the same time, there are some disquieting places in his conceptualizations. For instance, his disparagements of popular forms of preaching were quite biased. The writer's description of expositional preaching does not credit its inherent value. While he assesses expositional preaching as ineffective and irrelevant, if effectively prepared, an expositional sermon will in fact effectively address pain and deliver a message of hope. The truth is that expository preaching demonstrates scripture as the source of truth and the queen of human thought.

The author failed to note some inherent values in topical preaching. First, when topical sermons are delivered with attention to context, the effect is great. Second, if topical sermons are crafted

---

[87] Ibid., 19.

thoughtfully, they are excellent tools for addressing grief. Finally, as with expositional sermons, the effectiveness of topical preaching depends on the preacher.

Part 2.1.5 A Fifth Concept of Pastoral Preaching

Several concepts have been presented to the reader. Aden and Hughes contended for the sufferings of Christ. Powery, meanwhile, emphasized lament and celebration. Conversely, Nichols and Linn proposed models that were psychotherapeutic in nature. Both Nichols and Linn highlighted the scriptural text. All these concepts present equally necessary elements.

A final example of pastoral preaching is presented. Donald Hamilton wrote *Preaching with Balance* and therein distinguishes between pastoral and prophetic preaching. Pastoral preaching, he contends, contributes to the well-being of the listeners. Preaching that encourages, teaches, comforts, and guides further contributes to the well-being of listeners.[88]

In his perspective, pastoral preaching has various emphases, one of which is *preaching as counseling*. Hamilton says that preaching is effective as counseling when preachers engage in life-situational pulpit ministry. Wise preachers, he continues, exercise sensitivity when they address people's needs lovingly through the Word.[89]

Another emphasis in pastoral preaching is *preaching as exhortation*. Hamilton argues that while preaching as counseling gives direction in times of struggle, on the other hand, exhortation encourages

---

[88] Hamilton, Donald L. *Preaching with Balance*. (Ross-Shire: Christian Focus Publications, 2007): 183. Hamilton emphasizes the need for pastoral preaching as defined by the imagery in Luke 15.

[89] Ibid., 184.

people in times of despair. To illustrate, Hamilton explains that, in scripture, *exhort* is translated from *parakaleo*, (παρακαλέω) meaning literally, "to call a person to one's side."[90] The significance of this verbal illustration is that, in exhortation, the preacher comes to the side of the bereaved to bring a word of comfort.

Hamilton also emphasized *preaching with compassion.* Answers do not come easily when people grieve. Preachers should therefore focus on bringing hope rather than solutions. Ministers are oftentimes unaware of people's emotional dilemmas. Consequently, attempts to present solutions complicate the grief process. Therefore, assurance of God's presence and hope comes through scripture and through scripture alone.[91]

The final emphasis in pastoral preaching is *preaching with nurturing.* Describing nurturing sermons, Hamilton drew from John 21:15–17. In that passage, Jesus taught Peter to feed His sheep. In feeding the sheep, the preacher seeks to provide, nurturing their basic emotional, mental, and spiritual needs. Observe how Jesus enforced this principle:

> "So when they had dined, Jesus saith to Simon Peter, Simon, son of Jonas, lovest thou me more than these? He saith unto him Yea Lord; thou knowest that I love thee, He saith unto him, Feed my lambs. He saith to him again the second time, Simon, son of Jonas, lovest thou me? He saith unto

---

[90] Hamilton contends for a style of preaching known as "exhortation preaching." This style was based on the literal translation of παρακαλέω, which means *to call a person to the side* (Hamilton, *Preaching with Balance,* 186).

[91] Ibid., 188.

him, Yea Lord that I love thee, He saith unto him, Heed my sheep. He saith unto him the third time, Simon, son of Jonas, lovest thou me? Peter was grieved because he said unto him the third time, Lovest thou me? And he said unto him, Lord, thou knowest all things; knowst that I love thee. Jesus said unto him, Feed my sheep,"

Hamilton's perspective on pastoral preaching was rich with practical wisdom. First, the task of preaching pastorally is indeed a crucial element to pulpit ministry. Second, one's belief in the Word of God is furthermore indispensable to pastoral preaching. Third, it is essential that preaching convey the love and compassion of God.

Part 2.2 Pastoral Preaching Implemented

Various concepts of ministry were examined while examining the aforementioned concepts of pastoral preaching. These conceptualizations help further identify various perspectives on and approaches to pastoral preaching. In this next section, pastoral preaching is presented while demonstrating how various preachers employed it. For the sake of space, the research presents only a synopsis, rather than whole sermons.

Bryan Chapell, author of *The Hardest Sermons You Will Ever Preach,* compiles sermons related to various topics. Some are his sermons, while others are taken from contributors to his book. For example, he recalled a sermon in which Tim Keller targeted loss as it applied to a tragic death. On September 16, the Sunday following the events of September 11, 2001, Reverend Keller preached to a crowd of 5,100 emotional people. His chosen passage was John 11:1–44, where Jesus was portrayed weeping with Martha over Lazarus's death.[92]

Keller began by asking if Jesus could supernaturally remove Martha's pain. He responded that it was quite possible. Jesus, however, chose not to interrupt the means by which He created humans to process grief. Rather, He chose to participate in the grief through weeping with those who grieve.

Following this complex question, Keller then applied four aspects of Jesus's response to Lazarus's death to the events of September 11. Keller focused on Jesus's tears for Mary's pain. Then he emphasized Jesus's anger. Accentuating Jesus's anger also resonated with people's anger over the terrorist attacks in New York City. Next, he looked at the truth of Jesus, which lay in the hope for a future for those who suffer, especially for the victims of September 11.[93] Finally, Keller underscored the grace of Jesus. As the mighty counselor, Jesus is the counselor for people of the United States as He was for those at Lazarus's death.

As a pastor during September 2001, Chapell also felt compelled to respond to the 9/11 tragedies. He responded through the same passage Keller used.[94] Using John 11:1–44, he likewise compared the events of Lazarus's death with September 11. Chapell, however, constructed his homily around other scriptural truths from John 11.

---

[92] Bryan Chapell. *The Hardest Sermons You'll Ever Have to Preach.* (Nashville: Zondervan Publishing, 2011): 50.

[93] Keller in this section of his sermon rebuts the notion that people should get rid of the anger by letting it go. He argued that this is really not what Jesus intended for His followers to do with their anger at the death of Lazarus (Hamilton, *Preaching With Balance,* 50).

[94] Ibid., 61–70.

Chapell emphasized first that God foresaw the demise of Lazarus. Likewise, he proclaimed that while God through the Savior foreknew the events of Lazarus's death, He also foresaw the events of September 11, 2001. The second truth was that God understood what happened to Lazarus, just as He also understood the emotional effects surrounding the events of September 11. This knowledge of events meant for the mourners that God felt their pain. Third, God's triumph takes time. Death was not averted, but neither did that mean that God's purposes are uncertain. Finally, God's triumphs come in His time.

Chapell next presented an example of his own pastoral preaching while early in his tenure as chancellor at Covenant Theological Seminary. He was called to bring pastoral care amid another painful loss that involved an international student who was widely loved. Chapell chose Revelation 22:16[95] as his text, which reads: "I, Jesus, have sent mine angel to testify unto you these things in the churches. I am the root and the offspring of David, and the bright morning star."

Focusing on the name *morning star* as the core of his message, Chapell emphasized two distinctions about Jesus's name to comfort people. The first distinction is "what is precious?" This distinction accentuates how Jesus's name is a light of hope that darkness cannot conquer. The second distinction was "what is promised?" In its essence, light implies the dawn of another day. The dawn of another day was, therefore, the promise of hope in Jesus's name.

Dr. Robert Rayburn, pastor for Faith Presbyterian in Tacoma, Washington, presents another demonstration of pastoral preaching. The occasion involved a young man who died in a

---

[95] The title of Chapell's sermon was "What's in a Name?"

climbing accident, leaving behind a deeply grieving family.[96] In this particular case, Dr. Rayburn developed his message from different verses rather than one pericope.

Rayburn's first point in his message was that death was not outside God's will. Citing Psalm 139:16, he declared that one's days are ordered of the Lord. The author, therefore, urged the grieving family to find peace with God's deep wisdom. His next statement was that this particular death was not outside God's love. Notwithstanding the tragic demise, God's love was not diminished. The third aspect communicated that death was not outside of God's love for the victim, Joel. Emphasizing 2 Corinthians 5:8, Rayburn then encouraged the mourning congregation that the young man's final resting place was greater than anywhere on earth.[97]

Paul Tautges's *Comfort the Grieving* also presents an example of pastoral preaching. This sample, however, was not a funeral message like the previous examples. Rather, this sermon was delivered after the funeral. His message addressed a challenging question in the face of death: "Why are we here?"[98]

In response, Tautges presented key thoughts from Matthew 22:37–38, which reads, "Jesus said unto him, 'Thou shalt love the LORD thy God with all thy heart, with all thy soul, and with all thy mind. This is the first and great commandment.' " The first

---

[96] The title of Reverend Rayburn's sermon was "Seeing the Triumph in the Tragedy" (Hamilton, *Preaching with Balance,* 191).

[97] This was the first point to Chapell's sermon, which was aimed at breathing hope into the grieved.

[98] Paul Tautges. *Comfort the Grieving.* (Grand Rapids: Zondervan Publishers, 2014): 90–91. Interestingly, the sermon focused on assisting the collective grief of the congregation.

key point was that Jesus was humanity's substitute. The second point was that Jesus was humanity's atonement. The third key thought was that Jesus was humanity's redeemer.[99] Accentuating Jesus as humanity's substitute, atonement, and redeemer, Tautges accordingly declared humanity's created purpose. That purpose, he explained, was to serve and live for God.

Roger Alling and David Schlafer together offer sermon collections of various types. One such homily is presented by Reverend Mark Stanger at the funeral for an infant, who expired from sudden cardiac arrest. The main passage was Isaiah 66:7–14. From this passage, Stanger compared people's perspectives of life with certain famous images.[100]

In an effort to connect with the family, the minister opened with the natural tendencies of an infant. He explained that infants tend to look for images and wonder about them. Similarly, Stanger describes the imagery of intense suffering of the Jewish people while in captivity to the Babylonians.

Then, he portrayed the imagery of death taken from the window at Grace Cathedral in San Francisco. In the mural, though, there were words referring to death as a "gentle Sister."[101] Stanger's purpose was to illustrate death's inevitability and unpredictability. Finally, Stanger ended with the picture of the risen Christ and the promise that held for those who suffer. The picture, he explained, symbolized hope in eternal life. Stanger employed these images

---

[99] Ibid., 91.

[100] Roger Alling and David J. Schlafer. *Preaching as Pastoral Care: Sermons That Work XIII.* (Harrisburg: Morehouse Publishing, 2005): 1. The authors compiled sermon collections that speak to various issues related to bereavement.

[101] Mark Stanger's sermon was entitled *Pictures* because of the theme where the preacher's focus was on different spiritual lessons.

The Sunday after the Funeral

and the way people wonder about them with the way babies wonder about their own little worlds.

This section demonstrates how pastoral preaching is implemented in pastoral ministry. Samples from pastoral preaching are therefore submitted to illustrate foundational principles of pastoral preaching. These foundational principles such as relevance, comfort, and modeling were studied individually. The examination process also looked at how these principles contributed to the appropriateness and meaning of sermons to grieving congregations.

EXPOSITIONAL AND PASTORAL PREACHING

The preceding segments illustrated the significance of preaching as a modality of pastoral care to congregations that experienced traumatic loss. The first part, "Ministry of Pastoral Care," defined the art of pastoral care through various approaches and styles. The next part focused on pastoral preaching specifically. Both parts together presented the importance of conceptualization and implementation.

Part 3 studies scriptural exegesis and its contribution to pastoral preaching with two principal divisions. The first division explains expositional preaching from the perspectives of various professionals in homiletics. The second division examines the value of expositional preaching for pastoral care.

Part 3.1 The Practice of Expositional Preaching Explained

David Helm, a respected theologian and preacher in evangelical circles, explained expositional preaching. He argued that expositional preaching is critical to properly treating the text in proclaiming the gospel. Preachers, he continued, properly treat a given text when they magnify the Holy Spirit's inspiration. Giving voice and reverence to the Word of God, therefore, further enables the ministry of the Holy Spirit.

He also says that much of what has been defended as expositional preaching is not expositional in reality. Contextualization, for example, is often defended as expositional preaching. In reality, though, contextualization merely accentuates how the passage speaks to current experiences and times. The preacher's first responsibility to the passage, Helm contends, is to emphasize the historical and grammatical elements. These emphases must precede any further study and application of the passage.[102]

David Olford wrote a book entitled *Anointed Expository Preaching*. According to Olford, expository preaching emphasizes the explanation of the scriptures through the Holy Spirit's inspiration. He explains that in the process of exegesis, the preacher examines the historical, grammatical, and doctrinal nuances. These nuances then serve as the basis for exegesis.[103]

Dr. John MacArthur further explores the process in *Expository Preaching*. In expository preaching, the preacher focuses on one

---

[102] David Helm. *Expositional Preaching: How to Speak God's Word Today.* (Wheaton: Crossway Publishers, 2014): 9.

[103] Stephen F. Olford. *Anointed Expository Preaching.* (Nashville: B&H Publishing Group, 1998): 17–19.

main passage rather than several. MacArthur declares that the surrounding context of the passage is absolutely critical to proper exegesis.[104] He also explains that a sermon's direction is established through focusing on and developing one passage.

MacArthur then identifies five critical principles of expository preaching. First, scripture is the source of a sermon. Second, meticulous process of exegesis is critical to producing a message. Third, sermons must accurately interpret the scripture within the biblical context. The fourth component is the explanation of God's intended meaning from the passage. The final principle is the contemporary application of the passage. MacArthur presents these five principles as essential to biblical exposition.

In *Biblical Preaching*, Haddon Robinson explains and defends the art of expositional preaching in the church's ministry. He defines expository preaching as "the communication of a biblical concept, derived from and transmitted through a historical, grammatical and literary study of a passage in its context which the Holy Spirit first applied to the personality and experience of the preacher, then through the preacher applies it to the hearers."[105]

Robinson next presents his own perspective on expositional preaching. In developing his care, he declares that there are critical elements to expositional preaching.[106] First of all, the author contends that the passage should always govern the sermon. When

---

[104] John MacArthur. *Rediscovering Expository Preaching: How to Preach Biblically.* (Nashville: Thomas Neslon Inc., 2005): 19.

[105] Haddon W. Robinson. *Biblical Preaching.* (Grand Rapids: Baker Publishing Group, 2001): 20–21. Robinson argues in favor of expository preaching while giving attention to the grammatical and historical significances.

[106] Robinson emphasizes certain principles that are important to expositional preaching. 21–30.

Robinson expresses the term *governing,* he means that the sermon's idea and structure should arise from the scripture. Second, he says, the expositor communicates a concept to the hearers. Once again, the author has the scriptural concept in mind. The third essential element is the application of the concept to the hearers. These key points, Robinson explains, are necessary in crafting expositional sermons that speak effectively to human needs. Robinson contends that expositional preaching is not just *a* way of pastoral preaching, but it is *the* way.

Bryan Chapell, in *Christ-Centered Preaching,* also constructs a strong case for the practice of expositional preaching. He explains that expository preaching is the "attempt to present and apply the truths of a particular biblical passage." He continues by saying that expository preaching seeks to uphold three basic principles: the power of the Word, authority of the Word, and work of the Spirit. These same principles, Chapell argues, undergird true pastoral preaching.[107]

Two other well-respected theologians who defend expositional preaching are Leland Ryken and Todd Wilson in *Preach the Word.* In their work, they examine the art of expository preaching by studying the philosophies from different authors. In so doing, Ryken and Wilson then highlight various principles from their contributors. One of these principles is listening to the text. Listening to the text, they contend, is essentially just that—letting

---

[107] Bryan Chapell. *Christ-Centered Preaching.* (Grand Rapids: Baker Book House Company, 2004): 20. He insists that expository preaching is actually the only style that truly glorifies Christ.

the text speak, and allowing it to be the preacher's mentor and guide.[108]

Coupled with listening to the text is inductive study. The process of inductive research begins with grappling with the purpose and meaning of scripture.[109] Another important principle, they argue, is reading the Bible as literature, which means grasping the human experiences of the original authors of the Bible. These tasks, grappling with scripture and reading it as literature, are essential to performing an inductive study.

Part 3.1.2 The Value of Expositional Preaching Examined

Parishioners have historically considered preaching as much of a common activity in church as watching television is to the average family. That understanding, sadly, is disappearing as generations with vastly different understandings of preaching rise to adulthood. Scott Gibson edited a work entitled *Preaching to a Shifting Culture.* In it, he notes the distinct changes of opinion toward preaching. These changing opinions, Gibson explains, are also changing the face of preaching.[110]

A major challenge to preaching and expositional preaching, Gibson continues, is cultural relativism. Relativism asserts that there is no superior truth—essentially that one person's concept

---

[108] Leland Ryken and Todd Wilson. *Preaching The Word: Essays on Expository Preaching.* (Wheaton: Crossway Publishers, 2007): 40. They purport that expository preaching allows the passage to speak.

[109] By *grappling,* the author meant that the preacher should give close attention to the linguistic and historical significances of the passage even while preaching it. 14–17.

[110] Scott M. Gibson. *Preaching to a Shifting Curlture.* (Grand Rapids: Baker Publishing Group, 2004): 180.

of truth is as valid as anyone else's. This predominant belief is a direct challenge to the belief in the Bible as truth. Since biblical preaching is centered on the premise of a central truth, expositional preaching is therefore considered outdated.[111]

Paul Copan, in *True for You but Not for Me,* additionally emphasizes shifting social trends related to absolute truth. He points out that relativism is one of the social trends challenging contemporary preaching. He also notes that relativism is a mainstay for American thought. Its impact upon preaching is therefore profoundly negative, in his opinion, because people are increasingly skeptical of biblical truth.[112]

To illustrate, Barna Research Group conducted a survey in 2016 related to people's belief in scripture. They discovered that among born-again adults, a depreciation for scriptural inerrancy exists. Accordingly, they found that 44 percent of born-again adults believe in absolute truth.[113] This finding implies that a larger percentage of born-again adults do not believe in absolute truth, and this discovery sheds light into understanding the dilemma facing the art of preaching.

Keith Davis, in *Unbelief within the Church,* also contends that the art of preaching is not quite popular. In his book, Davis reveals that unbelief in truth has infiltrated churches. The corollary of this unbelief, he maintains, is the lack of the power of God in churches

---

[111] The writer reveals that relativism influences not only the manner in which people hear the Word but how they read it as well. Preaching, Scott says, is not connecting with the current culture. 180.

[112] Paul Copan. *True for You but Not for Me* . (Bloomington: Bethany House Publishers, 2009): 27–28.

[113] George Barna. http:www.pointofview.net/viewpoints. January 22, 2016 (accessed February 2, 2016).

today. Consequently, he writes that some people minimize the importance of preaching.[114]

In point of fact, some theologians consider the Bible as unessential to preaching. One such theologian is David Buttrick, who authored *A Captive Voice: The Liberation of Preaching.* He contends that the sermon need not begin with a scripture passage. In his estimation, scripture actually interferes with the practice of preaching and in fact detracts from the message that people actually need to hear.[115]

Buttrick's position is constructed on the premise that the Bible is not inerrant. In fact, he reasons that "the Bible rolls out of myth and winds up in eschatological vision." Buttrick also says that the Bible does contain meaning, although not in every passage. To substantiate his case, Buttrick argues that the Bible loses meaning because some passages are not even Christian. He in fact purports that preaching itself is a Word of God because any positive redemptive thought is inspired by the Holy Spirit.[116]

Another dissenting voice comes from Edwin Farley in *Ecclesial Reflection.* His comments regarding scripture mirror those of Buttrick, who claims that the Bible itself is errant as well as fallible; and Farley presents a similar sentiment. Farley claims that the Bible is not even divinely inspired. His central argument says that the bulk of the Bible is written by mere mortals—therefore,

---

[114] Keith Davis. *Unbelief within the Church.* (Greenville: Courier Publishing, 2015): 13.

[115] David Buttrick. *A Captive Voice: The Liberation of Preaching.* (Louisville: John Knox Press, 1994): 17. The writer contends that scripture can many times interfere with preaching effectively.

[116] Buttrick purported that oftentimes preachers cause greater injury when the scriptures are mishandled. (Buttrick, *Unbelief Within the Church,* 17).

their writings are not inspired. If the Bible is not inspired, Farley concludes, then it is not the Word of God.[117]

Part 3.1.2 The Value of Expositional and Pastoral Preaching Defended

These cultural shifts in opinion toward the Bible as truth profoundly affect the future of preaching. The question remains, then, is preaching—even expositional preaching, for that matter—irrelevant? Some people may in fact answer yes, as already seen. Others, however, embrace the fine art of expositional preaching and the Bible as truth. Clearly, the opposition is both forthright and unashamed. However, preaching—including expository preaching—should not be completely discounted, notwithstanding staunch opposition. Though the voices of dissention are vociferously bold, so are the voices of assent. In fact, those who assert the primacy of preaching and the centrality of the Word have a compelling case.

MacArthur, for instance, asserts the primacy of preaching. In fact, he stresses that the task of preaching is central to pastoral ministry. He cites, for example, how Paul admonishes his young protégé to preach the gospel. In 1 Timothy 4:1–4, Paul admonishes Timothy to place high importance on being ready to preach.[118] This admonishment is not simply a side note. Instead, it emphasizes what is most important and indispensable, preaching the Word.

Another advocate for biblical preaching is Calvin Miller. On the subject of the preacher and the shepherd, he writes, "Sermons are food, sheep food; and sheep who are not regularly fed become

---

[117] Edward Farley. *Ecclesial Reflection.* (Philadelphia: Fortress Press, 1982): 143.

[118] MacArthur also insists that preaching is the most important aspect to pastoral ministry (MacArthur, *Rediscovering Biblical Preaching,* 205).

restless and, in the furthest reach of the metaphor, begin to devour each other's wool."[119] He furthermore argues, "These sheep are not only unproductive, but they are often quarrelsome without understanding that they are merely hungry." In view of these comments, the purpose of preaching in the local congregations is as critical to the life of the people as is personal devotion. Additionally, he insists that preaching the scriptures is absolutely critical to the proper care of God's sheep.

Haddon Robinson also approaches the topic of preaching with highest regard. Arguing that while people have developed low regard for preachers, preaching is still essential. He also contends that pastors as shepherds have the calling to relate to their sheep in times of deep grief. Preachers must demonstrate how the Bible speaks to hopelessness, pain, grief, and suffering. They must furthermore demonstrate how the Bible speaks when they exposit the passages. Another contributing factor to this loss of importance is that modern society responds to mostly optical images. People also respond mostly to simple messages preached by televangelists.

Albert Mohler is a long-time champion for biblical preaching. In *Preaching: The Centrality of Scripture,* he categorically contends that preaching is preeminent in pastoral care. In the process, Mohler illustrates that Timothy's primary mentor in his life was scripture. Throughout church history, it was understood that Paul was Timothy's guide; but in truth, the Bible served as Timothy's

---

[119] Calvin Miller. *Preaching: The Art of Narrative Exposition.* (Grand Rapids: Baker Publishing Group, 2006): 25. Narrative expository preaching is where the preacher focuses on important aspects to a particular narrative.

guide.[120] The emphasis, therefore, focuses on Timothy's spiritual mentoring rather than on the one who mentored him.

Kyle Haseldon also maintains that preaching is critical to pastoral ministry. In *The Urgency of Preaching,* he presents two exhortations in order to restore the primacy of preaching. First, he contends preachers must have a renewed *passion* for preaching the Word. This renewed passion, he points out, is essential in light of the united front against conservative views of the Bible. Second, he insists the preachers must have a renewed *respect* for the power of preaching.[121] God designed people, Haseldon continues, to communicate and respond to communication. Preaching the Word, therefore, is the primary means for conveying a word from God.

CONCLUSIONS

This section of the project opened with the question, "What is the effectiveness of preaching as a modality of pastoral care?" Examination of the variety of resources related to pastoral ministry and preaching revealed serious considerations. First, ministers must consider preaching the Word of God as critical to pastoral care. This consideration was observed in MacArthur, Miller, Hamilton, and Frye, as well as others. Scholars also argue that the ministry of the Word of God is irreplaceable with psychology or "feel-good" theologies.

---

[120] Albert Molher. *Preaching: The Centrality of Scripture.* (Nashville: Thomas Nelson, 2005): 7. Mohler insists that it was in fact the Word that served as Timothy's guide and not Paul himself.

[121] Edward Farley. *Ecclesial Reflection.* (Philadelphia: Fortress Press, 1982): 31.

Second, research concluded that the efficacy of preaching lies in the relative source of pastoral care, one's heart. This conclusion ultimately says passion for the care of lives will invariably energize pastoral preaching. Teikmanis, Nicholes, Haseldon, and Olford all accentuated the need for passion in preaching.

Third, one's own perspective on the inspiration and inerrancy of scripture directs one's approach to preaching. This was clearly seen in Buttrick's and Farley's conclusions. Perceiving the Bible as a good resource is different from embracing it as the source of truth. MacArthur and Paul Copan both favored this perception. Scholarship also demonstrates how one's personal theological perspectives profoundly influence the way the Bible is approached homiletically.

Fourth, as demonstrated by Chapell's contributors, preaching the Word is divinely mandated. Most scholarship contended that preaching the Word is not only useful but also divinely mandated in pastoral care for grieving congregations. Pastors who do not give great attention to the practice of preaching are in fact disobedient to their call. Research further contended that preaching the Word is not a means that is dispensable. Rather, scholars argued that preaching the Word is in fact essential to ministering to grieving congregations.

Finally, the task of preaching brings a dynamic to pastoral ministry that is arguably a distinct way of providing pastoral care. Teikmanis, Hamilton, and MacArthur clarified this distinction. These authors demonstrated how preaching brings a ministry dynamic to caring for a grieving congregation that other means of pastoral support do not. Preaching as a means of pastoral care does not in any way devalue other aspects of pastoral care.

CHAPTER 3

The literature review studied various dynamics surrounding pastoral preaching. In the process, the researcher discovered how other scholars approached the topic academically. The major movements in the literature review were pastoral ministry dynamics, perspectives on scripture, the task of preaching, and the preacher's heart. The previous section, accordingly, established a literary basis for gathering scholarly information pertaining to pastoral preaching.

This next section, then, continues with the methodology utilized for gathering, interpreting, and presenting empirical information. As stated, this study seeks to examine pastoral care through preaching for congregations that have suffered traumatic losses. This section, then, examines the process of integrating empirical information with the research problem.

Ethical Considerations

An important consideration in all research projects is the ethical side. In the research process, therefore, the researcher must proceed with attention on right and wrong.[122] Otherwise, matters of trust and integrity of the research are compromised. This statement means that research students must always practice complete openness throughout the study and respect for the rights of the participants.

This research project will bring minimal risk to all participants involved. Participants in this study will consist of ministers who agree to be involved in the process. Permission from ministers, therefore, will be acquired prior to engaging in interviews, analysis of documents, observations, or questionnaires. Given the sensitive nature of the research, participation in the research is strictly voluntary. Ministers will provide information to the research process they deem necessary and least harmful.

The researcher will explain the nature and purpose of the study to all participating pastors. Pastors will have the freedom to withdraw from the research at any point. Furthermore, confidentiality concerning all materials, collected data, and participant identities is strictly observed throughout the process.

Selecting the Type of Research

Gary Thomas, in *How to Do Your Research Project,* identified two basic types of research approaches. The first is quantitative research,

---

[122] Gary Thomas. *How to Do Your Research Project.* (Los Angeles, Sage Publications: 2013): 37–38.

which typically studies large groups of people. Quantitative research begins with a theory and seeks to prove or disprove the theory. It uses deductive reasoning to resolve these theories. The researcher then gathers information and transposes it into statistics and percentages.[123] These figures and statistics are also implemented to demonstrate cultural shifts in opinion concerning a certain subject.

The second research approach is qualitative. Qualitative research, in contrast to quantitative, studies people's experiences. This examination of people's experiences is also known as empirical evidence. When seeking out empirical information, the researcher begins with research questions and utilizes information to deduce theories. The qualitative approach uses inductive reasoning.[124] The current research project seeks to understand pastoral preaching by drawing on the experiences of other pastors.

The type of method most compatible to this study, therefore, is qualitative research. John Creswell, in *Qualitative Inquiry and Design: Choosing among Five Approaches,* demonstrated that the qualitative approach places the researcher in the world. The researcher, he writes, "studies things in their natural settings, attempting to make sense of, or interpret, phenomena in terms of meanings people bring to them."[125] Qualitative research, then, places the researcher in the midst of his field of study. In one sense, the researcher is an observer, examining his subjects objectively. In another sense, though, the researcher is also a participant in the research.

---

[123] Thomas, *How to Do Your Research Project,* 116.

[124] Thomas, *How to Do Your Research Project,* 116.

[125] Creswell, *Qualitative Inquiry and Research,* 21.

The qualitative research approach is appropriate for several important reasons. First, it places the researcher as both an observer and a participant. For instance, this researcher serves as a local pastor and engages in a weekly preaching schedule. He is therefore personally concerned with preaching ministry. Second, the researcher engages in studying how other subjects participate in their respective roles. In this case, the researcher examines how other pastors preach pastoral messages to grieving congregations. Third, the qualitative approach allows the researcher to be an observer. The researcher in the current research project seeks opportunities to observe pastors in their preaching through recordings and documents.

SETTLING ON A RESEARCH STRATEGY

Out of all the types of research strategies, the phenomenological research strategy is most appropriate for this study. In conducting a phenomenological strategy, the researcher begins with a problem or a phenomenon as the heart of the research. Moreover, the phenomenological strategy draws from experiences of active preachers.[126] John Creswell wrote, "It describes the common meaning of several individuals of their lived experiences of a concept or phenomenon."[127] The phenomenon of preaching to grieving congregations is therefore the purpose of this study.

This strategy is appropriate because the researcher is seeking to understand how pastors approach pastoral preaching. More specifically, the researcher seeks to understand how pastors

---

[126] Ibid., 21.
[127] Ibid.

approach the task of preaching to grieving congregations following a tragic loss. In order to reach this understanding, the researcher intentionally avails himself of the experiences of other pastors. In doing so, the researcher satisfactorily resolves the research problem.

SYSTEMATIZING DATA COLLECTION METHODS AND RESEARCH QUESTIONS

Discovering the answer to research questions requires certain types of research methods. This exercise of discovering answers therefore involves synchronizing the appropriate collection method with the question. Oftentimes, the types of research methods used depend on the nature of the research question. There are also times when the same research method is utilized for several questions. Following is a list of research questions.

- How do the preacher's theological convictions inform the task of preaching to traumatized congregations?
- How is preaching the Word of God important to pastoral care for grieving congregations?
- How does the scriptural mandate to preach inform the task of preaching to grieving congregations?
- How does the preacher's heart attitude make preaching to grieving congregations effective?
- How is the task of preaching different from other ways of providing pastoral care to a grieving congregation?

To better facilitate the reader's grasp of the research, it is therefore helpful to explain the process of gathering information. Gary

Thomas, in *How to Do Your Research Project,* described several types of data-gathering techniques.[128] The first technique is the *questionnaire.* Questionnaires are useful tools for providing direction, structure, and ease in awkward situations. For the purposes of the current research, the questionnaire is a means of assessing the sample group. Questionnaires also aid in clarity and logic of interview questions.[129]

The second type of data-gathering technique Gary Thomas explained is the *interview,* which is a means of acquiring information through discussions. While he delineates various interview formats, one particular format is most appropriate for this research, the semi-structured interview.

We find three major benefits of the semi-structured interview in this process. First, the semi-structured format allows the researcher to ask open-ended questions while allowing the interviewee greater freedom. Second, the semi-structured format is tailored for use in small-scale research. Third, though the interviewee has more freedom in answering questions, there is still some structure during the interview.[130]

The final method for gathering information in the research process is *documentation interrogation.* Thomas explains that documentation interrogation involves the researcher studying important documents such as policies and technical guides.[131] Documentation interrogation involves studying sermon notes and other written materials deemed helpful to the participating pastor.

---

[128] Ibid., 191.

[129] Thomas also explained that the questionnaire had different uses, which expanded the possibilities of its utility in this research (Thomas, *How to Do Your Research Project,* 191).

[130] Thomas, *How to Do Your Research Project,* 198–199.

[131] Thomas, *How to Do Your Research Project,* 204–206.

For the purposes of this study, documentation interrogation will include certain approaches. First, reviewing participants' sermon notes and outlines will contribute to the research. Message notes delivered to congregations grieving from tragic losses are helpful in tracking the preacher's thought processes. Second, some ministers do keep personal diaries and meditation journals. These journals will also help the researcher understand the participant's spiritual and emotional journey throughout the event.

IMPLEMENTING RESEARCH

Implementation proceeded in the following manner. First, participants consisted of local church pastors who serve as either staff or senior ministers. Ministers chosen for this study were those who have dealt with or are currently dealing with a situation relative to the research. Pastors from congregations of various sizes were selected for the study process. The researcher acquired permission from ministers prior to the process.

Second, the researcher narrowed the number of participants in order to efficiently manage the study. With this narrowed focus in mind, the research process included six participants. Selecting six participants also facilitated accumulation of the type and necessary amount of data to achieve substantive research.

Third, the writer modified the methods of data collection according to feasibility. For the purposes of feasibility, the interviewer continued to reach out to participants until six participants were identified. Next, the researcher examined, organized, and presented data collected from the study. In order to strengthen the data field, the researcher acquired sermon notes from some of the participants.

SELECTING PARTICIPANTS

Several preparatory steps were taken prior to the research. First, the presenter compiled a list of participants from various sources, which included referrals through the South Carolina Baptist Convention staff and university faculty. Second, the researcher then obtained permission from participants for interviews. Third, the researcher explained the parameters of the study to each participating pastor. Based upon responses and recommendations from participants, the researcher modified and revised instrumentation. Next, the researcher scheduled appropriate times and dates for personal interviews with participants. Finally, the researcher conducted personal interviews with participants and gathered appropriate information.

INSTRUMENTATION OF DATA

Following is a construction of instrumentations utilized in the study.

Demographic Questions:

1. How long have you served in pastoral ministry?
2. How long have your served at your current church?
3. How many members regularly attend your church?
4. What is the average age of the members in your congregation?

5. How many traumatic losses (suicide, homicide, etc.) have occurred in your congregation?

6. What resources are available for dealing with a traumatic loss in your congregation?

7. Where did you receive your ministry training?

Questions for Interview:

1. What is your pastoral role in the congregation?

2. Please describe a traumatic event resulting in loss that caused grief in your congregation.

3. What do you remember most about that event?

4. What types of pastoral care did you deem appropriate at the time of the event?

5. How important is preaching as a means of pastoral care for grieving people?

6. To what extent did you address the event in a sermon following a funeral/memorial ceremony?

7. What were the thought/spiritual processes in deciding upon an appropriate preaching passage?

8. Describe the process in deciding an appropriate preaching topic.

9. Explain the sermonic approach you used in addressing the topic (direct, indirect, topical, expository, etc.).

10. When preaching to a grieving congregation, what recommendations would you give pastors?

11. How important is the Bible in ministering to grieving congregations?

INTERPRETATION OF DATA

Temporary constructs or themes are identified following the collection of data. This process of identifying themes follows several steps. First, there was a meticulous analysis of all the data. During the analysis, the researcher looked for significant juncture points in the material. These juncture points help identify possible main ideas. The researcher then searched for a repetition of these juncture points or ideas in the research material as well as for a rhythm revealed not only in the repetition of ideas, but also of dynamics related to the participant's pastoral preaching.

During the interview process, the interviewer listened for common themes in pastoral preaching. These themes included hope, encouragement, emotional pain, forgiveness, anguish, and at times anger. These repeated concepts were set apart from the rest of the material and served as directions for the research. Essentially, the participant's information, rather than the researcher's preconceived notions, guided the research.

Since interviews were the primary method of data gathering, the interviewer utilized a voice recorder, with permission of the participants. It was a challenge, however, to convert recorded discussions into printed documents. To overcome this challenge, the researcher found a program called Google Voice. Google Voice enabled the interviewer to convert interviews into printed material while listening to the recorded conversations and simultaneously speaking into the computer microphone to produce manuscripts of the interviews.

Second, the researcher implemented a reference system in order to identify major themes in the transcriptions, which was important in order to organize the process of information gathering. To simplify the process, the researcher employed color coding. Using the *text highlight color* tab, the researcher employed various colors to identify major constructs. A lower order of codification is also implemented to identify *second-order constructs,* which are discussed next.

Throughout the process, the researcher looked for developmental patterns within the main ideas. These patterns thus revealed subthemes or second-order constructs. These, Thomas explained, clarify temporary constructs or main ideas. These subthemes also help the reader find direction, structure, and clarity in the interpretation process. Again, the researcher used the text highlight tab to identify second-order constructs or subthemes.

Fourth, the writer examined the data for unrelated concepts. Thomas called these unrelated concepts *counter examples.*[132] Counterexamples are pieces of information that do not necessarily flow with the major themes. Although counterexamples at times seem irrelevant in constructing major themes, they are, however, significant to interpreting the minister's story. In terms of pastoral preaching, *counterexamples* reflected features such as family dynamics, shifts in people's spirituality resulting from the events, and redefining the pastor's relationship with the congregation. The researcher will elaborate more on these counter examples in chapter 4.

---

[132] Ibid., 204–205.

PRESENTATION OF DATA

The researcher presented temporary constructs, counterexamples, and second-order constructs in his own words. In order to further assure confidentiality of participants, the researcher also employed nongendered language. Throughout the presentation section, the presenter inserted quotations from participants as much as possible to substantiate findings.

Data was subsequently organized according to the participants' experiences with preaching to grieving congregations. The researcher's goal, therefore, was to present information based upon empirical data rather than assumptions or conjecture. Initially, the presenter sought to emphasize themes rather than the participants. In the course of the research, however, the presenter observed that the participants' personal reactions to the events revealed important dynamics. Consequently, the presenter will speak at length to these dynamics in chapter 4.

CHAPTER 4

T his chapter is multi-tiered. In the first part of the chapter I will outline important demographic features about the respondents and the churches. Then, I will present some brief descriptions of each scenario researched. Next, I will examine the homiletical strategy practiced by the pastors. Following homiletical strategies, chapter 4 explores how participants utilized homiletics to engage grief and reinforce pastoral care. Finally, this chapter will conclude with homiletical approaches of each pastor in the study. I will expound on each contextual characteristic below.

The research proceeded with three empirical unknowns, supported by five research questions. As previously identified, an empirical unknown is information that is available only through field research and fashioned into a question. In this project, the field interviews addressed each empirical unknown from various perspectives. These empirical unknowns and research questions are likewise treated systematically.

In order to answer the empirical unknowns, the presenter

carefully constructed certain interview questions, which achieved two goals accordingly. First, they focused on certain areas of preaching pertinent to pastoral care following a traumatic event. Second, they captured data that examined the necessity of post-trauma preaching. The interview questions, therefore, gave voice to the research questions and provided direction for the overall study.

From the outset, the researcher planned to gather information primarily through interviews and secondarily through surveys. Field research proved, however, that ministers were more open to responding to personal interviews than to surveys. Consequently, the researcher found personal interviews were more fruitful and accommodating to pastors than surveys. The research subsequently did not utilize surveys. The research relied on data gained through interviews and demographic studies. In addition, research utilized sermon outlines and manuscripts as documentation interrogation.

Conducting interviews with pastors who have walked with people during painful experiences was an emotionally moving process. Often during the interviews, the participants and interviewer grieved together. In order to ensure that preconceived notions did not overshadow the research, the presenter utilized a semi-structured format with open-ended questions. Throughout the interview process, however, the researcher intermittently revised interview questions. These revisions stemmed from the directions taken in each successive dialogue.

Second, the interviewer adjusted discussions for accuracy according to respondents' recommendations. In the course of investigating tragedies, for example, item number two was inadequate in capturing essential information. Item two read,

"Please describe a traumatic event resulting in loss that caused grief in your congregation." In the process of the interviews, this discussion item did not elicit helpful information. The interviewer, therefore, reframed the statement to ask about pastoral care interventions necessary following the trauma events.

FIRST CONTEXTUAL CHARACTERISTIC: DEMOGRAPHICS OF PARTICIPANTS

From the beginning, respondents intentionally excluded certain aspects of the events from the interviews. This agreement was to ensure the anonymity of victims, the families, the congregations, and the pastors themselves. In some cases, active investigations by local authorities were ongoing. Any disclosure of sensitive information would potentially jeopardize active investigations and upset the lives of parties involved.

During the study, the interviewer discussed certain demographic features with the pastors. These features essentially constructed the foundation for each pastor's ministry context. The types of demographic information explored with each participant were basic biographical aspects of their lives and ministries (see table 1). Research, then, implemented these data to determine correlations between prior events and the event discussed in the interviews.

The researcher interviewed each pastor according to four pieces of demographic information. This demographic data consisted of years of ministry experience, prior trauma experiences, highest level of formal education, and trauma/intervention training received. The shaded areas of table 1 present the type of experience and training/education each pastor received. The outer boxes represent the ratio between those who possessed said experiences/ education and those who did not. For example, the upper-left quadrant contrasts the ratio of respondents who received trauma-related training and those who did not—indicating that three out of six respondents received trauma-related training.

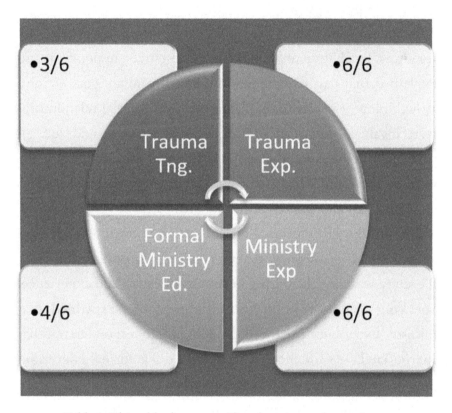

Table 1: This table shows specific education and experience of the pastors.

This information led to several interesting observations. First, each of the pastors possessed over twenty-five years of ministry experience. This experience allowed these ministers to respond effectively to their trauma situations with resources ready at hand. These resources included Bible-study tools, Bible knowledge, homiletical resources, and the ability to empathize. Participants also testified how ministry experience spawned spiritual and emotional maturity, which served them well.

Second, each pastor reported having a significant degree of experience with pastoral intervention in prior traumas. Even though respondents explained that all trauma situations are different, previous experiences provided them with knowledge and resources. In addition to knowledge and resources, respondents also explained that past experiences produced ministry connections. What's more, each pastor explained that ministerial relationships were invaluable personal and professional assets. In addition, all participants contended that the relationships were of inestimable value to their ministries.

Third, all the pastors received formal theological training. Moreover, the participants also elaborated on how their education assisted them in ministry. Another interesting observation from the study was the relationship between education and experience. Speaking to this relationship, all the pastors explained that ministry experience enhanced their abilities to respond to traumas appropriately. As for those who possessed less formal education, they described experience as their teacher.

Fourth, the study revealed that all the pastors had strong pastoral relationships with parishioners. In terms of strong pastoral relationships, the pastors described how their relationship with their parishioners contributed considerably to their abilities to provide crisis intervention. One of the ways this pastoral relationship contributed to their ministries was trust. For example, one pastor explained that parishioners lean on their pastor when they trust him. A pastoral relationship is not assumed; it is created.

Finally, the pastors furthermore explained that these events created opportunities for relationships with local agencies. The relationships were invaluable during the events and during the weeks following the events. Some of the agencies with which pastors built relationships as a result of the events were police, emergency response, counselors, and even other faith groups. Relationships with these agencies were constructive resources for the participants and their church communities as well. In fact, all the respondents suggested that other pastors build such relationships before trauma events occur.

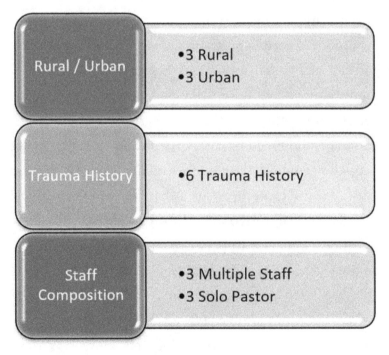

Table 2 presents three areas of church demographics.

DEMOGRAPHICS OF CHURCHES

During the study, the researcher examined churches and their pastors (see table 2). Regarding church demographics, the study examined aspects that contributed to understanding the impact of the traumas. The research, however, excluded some of the demographic data such as average age and average attendance. A few respondents chose not to go into great detail. Table 2 respectively depicts churches according to context, staff composition, and trauma history.

For example, all the churches examined experienced losses due to traumatic events prior to the event studied. This history of trauma produced certain posttraumatic reactions. Respondents to the study all lamented that they and their parishioners experienced these posttraumatic reactions. Respondents also explained that memories and emotions that characterized these reactions sometimes compounded pastoral care during current events.

Regarding context, the churches studied were divided evenly. One distinct difference between urban and rural churches was accessibility to certain resources. In urban settings, for example, congregations were less dispersed, and communication was not as hampered. Another difference was that rural congregations typically separated from associational staff and resources. This separation sometimes produced feelings of isolation.

Another feature observed during the study was the staff composition of the churches. Initially, the study sought to assess churches with only one pastor. Finding churches with only one pastor willing to participate in the study proved difficult. Certain adjustments to the project's boundaries were necessary. The research focus was broadened accordingly to incorporate multi-staff churches into the study (see table 2).

With respect to staff composition, the study revealed certain interesting data. First, churches with only one pastor depend heavily upon that pastor in times of distress. In churches with multiple staff members, the responsibilities of pastoral care were shared. Consequently, emotional burnout was a major concern for all participants, but especially for solo pastors.

Second, pastors who served alone often saw the need to broaden their training and experience. Most participants responded that the specialized trauma education they received arose from past trauma experiences. The research discovered that two of the six participants sought out more training to enhance their knowledge and capabilities.

SECOND CONTEXTUAL CHARACTERISTIC: DESCRIPTION OF SCENARIOS

Each event is described briefly in this section. Due to the sensitive nature of the events themselves, only a few details are provided. As explained previously, the descriptions of the scenarios are brief, since investigations are still ongoing in some cases. In other cases, the respondents restricted the type and amount of information they shared. The following scenarios entail four reportable features. These features are the type of death, approximate age of the deceased, the pastor's interventions, and approximate congregation size.

Timothy S. Thompson

Scenario One

Scenario one involved the tragic death of a teenager in her mid-teens. The cause of death was vehicular. Hearing of the accident, the pastor immediately responded with crisis intervention for the family. The pastor next described how this type of event traumatized the entire congregation of about sixty-five worshippers.

Scenario Two

In scenario two, the situation involved the tragic death of a young teenager in a congregation of 180 parishioners. Although a little different from the preceding tragic event, this event produced similar dynamics. The teenager suffered significant pulmonary obstructions that increased rapidly during a youth event. The teenager subsequently died. Hearing of the event, the pastor reported that he immediately proceeded to the hospital. The pastor explained how he next intervened with emotional and spiritual counseling.

Scenario Three

The next two scenarios involve churches that experienced deaths due to homicides. The third scenario involved a relational struggle between two young teenagers that resulted in a homicide. Hearing about the event, the pastor proceeded immediately to the deceased's home. Once there, the pastor explained, he provided crisis intervention for two traumatized parents. The pastor then expounded how deeply the event affected his congregation of 130 constituents.

Scenario Four

Due to the highly sensitive nature of this scenario, the respondent asked to keep the details brief. Essentially, the event involved the tragic homicide of a child in a parish of 280 active members. During the event, the pastor explained that he focused most of his energy in crisis intervention for the parents and concerned parties. As a means of emotional support, the pastor conducted stress debriefings for parishioners and relatives of the deceased.

Scenario Five

The last two scenarios entailed deaths resulting from suicide. In the fifth scenario, the pastor reported that a teenager died from a self-inflicted gunshot wound to the head. As in the previous scenarios, the pastor responded by immediately going to the family's side. Pastoral support, the respondent explained, involved prompt crisis and emotional support. With painful recollection, the pastor then explained how this event deeply moved his congregation of around four hundred.

Scenario Six

The final scenario involved the death of a young teenager. He died from hanging himself. As in many other terrible stories, the parents came home to find their lifeless child in their home. The event occurred in a small Hispanic congregation of about fifty parishioners. This particular event, the pastor reported, absolutely traumatized the congregation. The pastor related that he responded promptly to the family's side to provide emotional and crisis intervention.

THIRD CONTEXTUAL CHARACTERISTIC: HOMILETIC STRATEGY

As stated, the purpose of this research is to understand how pastors employ preaching as a means of pastoral care in times of traumatic loss. Previously, the research presented individual case studies involving traumas. At this point, the research focuses on each pastor's homiletic strategy. The guiding question for homiletic strategy is the first empirical unknown. It investigates the value of preaching in providing pastoral care to a congregation that has suffered a tragic loss.

Each subsection will respond to the first empirical unknown from a different perspective. These perspectives explore pastoral involvement, homiletic strategy components, listening to the Holy Spirit, and primacy of preaching. Each subsection, in addition, will respond to the first research question. The first research question accordingly explores the preacher's theological convictions as they inform the task of preaching to traumatized congregations.

Pastoral Involvement

Nothing replaces the role of the pastor in the local church. All the respondents echoed this conviction, noting how these events reinforced the importance of their roles. This subsection in particular emphasizes listening to grieving parishioners. Most of the pastors substantiated the importance of the pastor's ministry with Ephesians 4:11–13, which reads,

> "And He gave some, apostles; and some prophets; and some evangelists; and some, pastors and teachers; for the perfecting of the saints, for the work of the ministry, for the edifying of the body of Christ: till we all come in the unity of the faith, and of the knowledge of the Son of God, unto a perfect man, unto the measure of the stature of the fullness of Christ."

During the conversations, respondents reported that an important piece of pastoral care was dialogue—one that must transpire between the grieving parishioner and the pastor. All the pastors interviewed contended that in order to know where people are emotionally, the pastor must visit. The primary task in visits, they noted, was listening to the tough questions, the heart-wrenching stories, and the emotional expressions. These places of deep emotional and spiritual anguish revealed where people required support.

Another important piece to involvement is relationships. The pastors explained that ministers in general must work at building relationships with their congregants. In fact, participants reported that these relationships enable them to provide meaningful care in time of need. These relationships, they added, laid the foundation of trust that facilitated open dialogue with grieving parishioners. In terms of providing effective pastoral intervention in times of trauma, the pastor's involvement with and listening to parishioners is indispensable.

As one pastor explained, "You have to earn the right to be heard." He went on to justify his statement by explaining that just because one is the pastor, people will not arbitrarily listen to him. He has to earn this right to be heard in times of trauma. This right derives from a pastoral relationship that is painstakingly carved out of faithful visitation. Moreover, it is incumbent upon all ministers in a multi-staff context that they establish individual pastoral relationship with congregants.

Listening to the Holy Spirit

Listening to parishioners is necessary to understanding their grief. Another important theological conviction that inspired the homiletic strategies was listening to the Holy Spirit. One pastor explained, "If you don't listen to the Spirit, you won't know what to say." All of the respondents interviewed reported that listening to the Holy Spirit is essential to having a timely message from God. One pastor commented from 2 Chronicles 7:14 to illustrate how people must pray and seek after God's direction. It reads, "If my people which are called by name shall humble themselves and pray, and seek my face, and turn from their wicked ways; then will I hear from heaven, and will forgive their sin, and will heal their land."

More to the point, respondents testified to the primary means of listening to the Holy Spirit as being prayer. Respondents accordingly described how they waited for God's voice in providing effective pastoral intervention. In point of fact, all the participants explained how an active prayer life was indispensable. Shepherding God's sheep, they continued, requires direction from the Shepherd Himself. The respondents, therefore, explained that prayer and reading scripture were the main avenues of hearing from God.

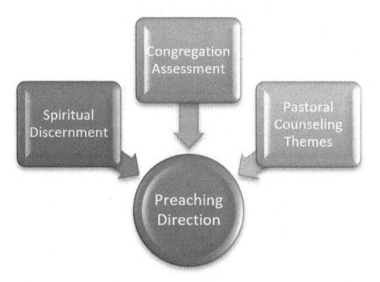

Table 3 examines the components of homiletic strategies and how they support preaching directions.

Components in a Homiletics Strategy (Table 3 and inscription on this page)

The discussions produced some fascinating insights regarding homiletic strategy components. Table 3 illustrates accordingly the three components each respondent reported as paramount in a post-trauma homiletic strategy. As depicted in the first block of the diagram, all respondents reported that the first component was spiritual discernment.

Spiritual discernment, they also believed, consisted of

prayer and meditating on the Word of God. A pastor is able to receive a word from God when he is spiritually discerning. This sentiment was a commonly shared conviction among respondents that all pastors must seek the Lord's guidance before preaching. Respondents also clarified that spiritual discernment is a process and not a skill. It consists of allowing the Lord to speak through various media such as music and scripture.

The second component was congregational assessment. Each pastor indicated that, in addition to listening to the Lord, one must listen to the people. Listening to people also implies a presence with people. Of course, one of the ways in which the pastor is most visibly present with his people is through visitation. While present with their people, the respondents continued, they sought to hear what was said during the visits, as well as what was left unsaid or simply implied.

The final component in the post-trauma homiletic strategy was preaching direction. All pastors, respondents contended, must have a word that speaks to a grieving people where they are at the moment. Discerning the Lord's inspiration, assessing congregational climate, and considering counseling themes contribute to preaching direction. Table 3, then, conveys the process of preaching following a traumatic event. Speaking of this process, respondents stressed that ministers must not engage in homiletic intervention haphazardly. The process requires time and great attention to various facets of pastoral intervention.

The Primacy of Preaching

Hearing from God is paramount in times of trauma. When people are suffering, a word from God is critical, and pastors are called to communicate that word. Respondents all deeply believed that the primary mode of communicating a word from God was preaching. As important as counseling and small group support are in pastoral care, respondents still described preaching as essential. Moreover, respondents described preaching as the preferred method of intervention. Parishioners, the respondents explained, sought after a word from their pastors in those painful times.

Preaching was considered paramount, because it was the method by which one mainly receives a word from God. The Bible, according to all respondents, was the centerpiece in their pastoral care. As one respondent exclaimed, "Without the Word of God, I have nothing to say!" This statement also characterized the sentiments of other respondents. Hearing of the traumas, all respondents reported that they consulted the Word to find direction and inspiration for the rest of their intervention. It was the orienting piece that guided them from the beginning and throughout the process of caring for their flocks.

One final thought is presented regarding the primacy of preaching. During the interviews respondents expounded on their beliefs concerning scripture. More specifically, they explained their modes of preaching the Bible. When asked, four out of six respondents explained that expository preaching was their method of choice. In other cases, the respondents were quick to add that they often utilized a mixture of preaching methods. These other oft-employed methods were topical and contextual, which is a form of expositional preaching.

For the most part, respondents defended expositional preaching because it more accurately illuminated scripture. Expositional preaching, they further explained, was the process of examining a passage in a systematic verse-by-verse study. All the while, they accentuated significant grammatical and contextual elements in their sermons. Regardless of their particular positions on expositional preaching, all the respondents held strong convictions about scripture's authority. Particularly, scripture is authoritative when ministering to grieving people.

FOURTH CONTEXTUAL CHARACTERISTIC: DYNAMICS OF HOMILETIC INTERVENTION

The preceding section expounded the necessity of pastoral involvement, listening to the Spirit, homiletic strategy components, and primacy of preaching. All these subjects defined the strategies pastors employed while responding to traumatic losses. This next section addresses the second empirical unknown that asks, "What is the extent to which preaching is utilized as a means of pastoral care?" The second and third research questions, accordingly, support this unknown. They ask respectively, "How is preaching the Word of God important to pastoral care for grieving congregations?" and "How does the scriptural mandate to preach inform the task of preaching to traumatized congregations?"

Likewise, this section will explore the third empirical unknown that seeks to know the relationship between pastoral support and preaching following a tragic loss in the congregation.

The fourth and fifth research questions, in turn, support this unknown. They ask how the preacher's heart attitudes influence preaching to traumatized congregations effectively and how the task of preaching is distinct from other ways of providing pastoral support to grieving congregations.

Dominant Themes in Homiletic Intervention

The study examined six churches. In the process, the presenter spoke with pastors who experienced suicides, homicides, and tragic deaths. In order to balance the results, the presenter partnered with two churches from each major area. Examining each area individually also honored the distinct grief elements in each type of trauma.

Conversations with respondents also unveiled some major themes in their homiletic interventions. These preaching themes address the second empirical unknown (see table 4). They furthermore speak to the second research question, which investigates how preaching the Word of God is important to pastoral care. In so doing, they also amplify the third research question. The third research question, then, explores how the scriptural mandate to preach informs the task of preaching to traumatized congregations. Table 4 therefore shows the relationship between the major area studied and the dominant preaching themes of each area.

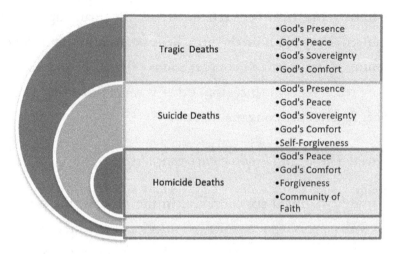

Tragic Deaths	•God's Presence •God's Peace •God's Sovereignty •God's Comfort
Suicide Deaths	•God's Presence •God's Peace •God's Sovereignty •God's Comfort •Self-Forgiveness
Homicide Deaths	•God's Peace •God's Comfort •Forgiveness •Community of Faith

Table 4: This table displays each major area and dominant preaching themes.

Pastors who dealt with suicides and tragic deaths all reported some common themes. In some cases, preaching themes varied according to event specifics. Some of the common themes, though, were God's comfort, peace, and presence. All the pastors explained that one of the prevailing emotions survivors of a suicide expressed was guilt. One respondent in particular explained how the Bible was the only source of true comfort for people dealing with such guilt. He referred to Ecclesiastes 3:3–4, which says, "To everything there is a season, a time to every purpose under Heaven, a time to weep and a time to laugh and at time mourn and a time to dance."

As stated above, comfort was a predominant theme. Whether the event involved a suicide, homicide, or tragic accident, comfort was essential. What is more, all the respondents reported that the message of comfort was predominant even in pastoral visits. Despite the fact that pastors may provide that comfort through private counseling sessions, nothing replaces scripture. When conveying comfort through scripture, all respondents looked to the scriptures for guidance in demonstrating how Jesus comforted those who grieved.

Another important theme was peace. People wrestling with intense emotional turmoil due to traumas like the ones studied rarely recover immediately. This turmoil affects other aspects such as relationships, work, hobbies, and literally every part of a person's life. Respondents reported that mourners experienced difficulty concentrating and thinking rationally following a tragic loss.

The pastors accordingly discovered the necessity of addressing these upsetting experiences especially through scripture. Peace, they explained, was a theme that the Holy Spirit placed in their minds and hearts. Mourners struggle to find perspective following traumatic loss and frustrate themselves in the endless pursuit of answers. However, all of the pastors interviewed reported that the Word of God spoke peace when all other means failed.

Two other themes were God's presence and His sovereignty. The respondents concluded from their experiences that mourners needed to know God was with them. Although sometimes taken for granted, this assurance was not clearly sensed. Participants also explained that grieving families all testified to a sense of detachment from spiritual anchors that once kept them stable. In addition, respondents recounted that the Holy Spirit confirmed that a focus on God's sovereignty was also appropriate. Intense grief following a tragic loss spawned questions of faith and pain. Pastors then felt led to reinforce people's trust in Christ through God's sovereignty.

Those ministers who dealt with homicides identified certain

unique themes. For example, they reported that an emphasis on community of faith was helpful. The concept of community of faith, each pastor explained, reminded everyone that not only do families grieve, but so does the whole body. Consequently, an effective and appropriate intervention was necessary, preaching.

In addition to the community of faith, forgiveness was another important theme. Anger and intense loss, respondents reported, often collided within the hearts of mourners. This collision of anger and intense loss consequently impeded God's peace. In terms of intense loss, mourners reported that they felt cheated or robbed of someone precious to them. By and large, pastors immediately focused on the necessity of forgiveness in their preaching. They proceeded, of course, with the understanding that forgiveness is a painstaking process. They furthermore clarified that forgiveness was more for the mourner than for the perpetrator. Even in times of suicide, self-forgiveness was necessary.

Interestingly, the types of deaths each church experienced involved the death of a minor. Although the research was not planned this way, it introduced an additional set of dynamics. The first of these dynamics was the effects upon family units. Emotional grief due to suicide or homicide is different from death by natural causes. In the case of child demise, entire families and congregations feel the trauma. In most cases, pastors reported that the grief process continued for years after the event. This intense emotional upheaval and prolonged grieving process were determining factors for knowing what to say and where to begin.

Another dynamic reported was the effect of a child's demise upon the ministers. Pastors are clay vessels empowered by the Holy Spirit. When a child dies, therefore, pastors feel the emotional impact as well. It was also reported that some ministers bear a certain degree of personal responsibility regarding the loss. This personal responsibility is especially true for pastors who participated in the child's spiritual journey. Respondents reported that they were involved in the child's journey through baptism, conversion, and mentorship.

A final dynamic was the effect upon communities. Children, like their parents, build relationships in the community. When these connections are suddenly severed, emotional separations take place. Pastors reported that one of their pastoral interventions, therefore, involved intervention in the community. As with congregations and families, the grief process for communities often endures. That being said, so does the pastoral care.

Major Pastoral Tasks of Intervention

Respondents also identified certain tasks necessary to providing effective and timely interventions. These tasks are ministry through the scriptures, mobilization of the congregants, and coordination with resources (see table 5). This subsection illustrates the third empirical unknown, which subsequently investigates the relationship between preaching and pastoral support (see table 5).

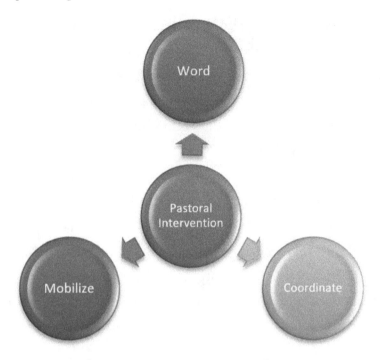

Table 5 outlines common tasks in pastoral interventions.

Table 5 outlines how these tasks defined the respondents' pastoral intervention. This diagram respectively displays how these pastoral tasks are, in one sense, distinct from preaching, illustrating the fifth research question. In another sense, however, the table shows how all these tasks support pastoral intervention. The fifth research question, therefore, examines the distinction between preaching and other tasks of pastoral care.

One main task was mobilization of congregants. The pastors explained that mobilizing people to care for mourners was often expressed through preaching. In the process of mobilization, pastors also intentionally rallied support around grieving families. These rallies of support contributed to building grief networks within the congregations. In some cases, respondents reported that mobilization was also self-initiated in congregations. In other cases, it was facilitated through preaching.

Another important task identified was coordination. The table shows a twofold connection. First is the connection between the pastor and the church in terms of regular visitation. Then, there is the connection as it applies to connecting grieving families with resources. For instance, one respondent presented an outline from a preaching series in which he urged people to grieve and, if necessary, seek support. In some cases, respondents worked with outside agencies in counseling and caring for the grieving victims.

The first and most important task identified was ministry through the Word. This function of pastoral care was critical. As mentioned in the previous section, preaching was considered paramount and irreplaceable. The task of preaching was subsequently placed at the top of the table (see table 5). All respondents furthermore contended that pastoral intervention was incomplete without preaching. Table 5, therefore, demonstrates how coordination of resources and mobilization support the ministry of the Word.

Preaching accentuates some important practical support elements for a grieving congregation. One of these support elements is admonishment. One pastor explained that when dealing with a homicide death, he felt led by the Holy Spirit to emphasize the community of faith. In so doing, he admonished members through his preaching to fill a role in ministry to grieving families. His emphasis further contributed to the task of church mobilization.

In addition, respondents noted that their preaching accentuated coordination. Coordination seeks to connect mourners with resources. Pastors also explained that their messages brought clarity and understanding to tough questions. Bringing clarity to these questions, therefore, enabled parishioners to empathize with grieving people. Preaching not only opened the door for empathy, but also showed parishioners how to intervene effectively.

Finally, this subsection also speaks to the heart attitudes of the pastors themselves, the fourth research question. In each case, the respondents explained how these situations inspired and challenged them. Seeing people in pain moved these pastors to action. This move to action, respondents explained, arose from a sense of responsibility and love. People needed a pastor to intervene, and all the pastors explained that the need invited opportunities to minister.

Another heart attitude was a willingness to suspend their personal lives. They all expressed that these extreme situations also produced some extreme challenges as well. In one particular case, a pastor explained how a situation involving a suicide required his presence for three days. He spent three days physically in the hospital with the family. Being a bi-vocational pastor, this challenge also required negotiation with his supervisor at work. Not only did the event pull him away from work, but it pulled him from his family as well. When asked how he felt about these challenges, he replied that it was his calling.

In addition to a sense of responsibility and the sense of call was the sense of human connection. In short, human connection means empathy. All respondents expounded on their abilities to relate to their people. God, they clarified, called them to serve as undershepherds. Their being fathers, sons, brothers, and husbands themselves made the events personal. They placed themselves in the places of pain that the mourners experienced and imagined how it felt. Their heart attitudes inspired these pastors to intervene and moved them to action.

FIFTH CONTEXTUAL CHARACTERISTIC: HOMILETIC DIRECTIONS

In the previous section, the research focused on homiletic themes and pastoral care tasks related to three major events: tragic deaths, suicides, and homicides. Those two subsections respectively demonstrated the dynamics of homiletics in post-trauma intervention. This next section examines the homiletic directions that the participants considered appropriate for their respective congregations. These homiletic directions are subsequently divided into main subject groups: homiletic campaigns and homiletic approaches. In terms of the flow of research, this section on homiletic directions supports the third empirical unknown.

Homiletic Campaigns

In terms of homiletic campaigns, the research focuses on three considerations. These considerations accordingly depict the timing, duration, and nature of preaching (see table 6). The first of these considerations involved the timing. This timing refers to a preaching campaign that was either immediate or delayed following the event. By *immediate,* the point is that some preachers address the event immediately following the funeral. Delayed, of course, refers to a delayed treatment of the event in sermons following the funeral. Second, there was the duration of preaching. This consideration refers first to a preaching duration that was sustained over a period of weeks. The other type of duration refers to a limited address of the subject in worship services following the event. Then, there was the nature of preaching. This final consideration speaks to a preaching campaign that employed expository preaching or other types of preaching methods.

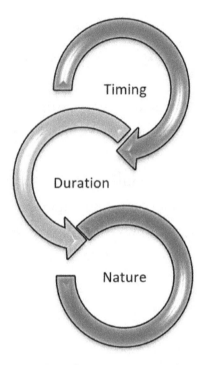

Table 6 illustrates homiletic campaigns of respondents.

Table 6, therefore, illustrates these individual considerations. The first of these considerations explains the participants' preaching campaign is immediate versus delayed. Describing the timing aspect, the researcher discovered that respondents had differences of opinion. Research found that two out of six respondents waited for a short period of time, two or three weeks, before engaging the event homiletically. Their reasons for waiting were, first of all, to allow the initial shock from the event to settle in the congregation.

Second, waiting before addressing the event homiletically allowed opportunities to provide triage for families. Providing triage for the family basically entailed first responder bereavement intervention. Third, pastors also purported that waiting before they addressed the event after the funeral allowed them more time to determine where to begin.

In terms of duration, there were again differences of perspective from respondents. On the average, pastors who engaged the traumatic event immediately did so for about four weeks. Participants reported that engaging the event homiletically for that timeframe was a preventive measure. Respondents also explained that prolonged attention on a painful situation was often counterproductive. That is to say, prolonged attention interfered with the grief cycle.

Another consideration in the preaching campaigns was the style of preaching. In terms of style, the emphasis is on expository preaching versus other methods such as topical. Three of the six pastors interviewed, in fact, reported that they preached expository messages in times of trauma. This ratio, therefore, illustrated a divided opinion. At the same time, though, some respondents reported that they often utilized expository and other methods in their preaching campaigns.

Related to expository preaching is the question of direct versus indirect preaching. Regarding direct versus indirect preaching, the emphasis centered on directly addressing the loss or referring to it in general terms. Most respondents explained that they preferred the indirect method of engaging the trauma publicly. Predominantly, their reasons were similar. They reported that direct engagement of the subject will sometimes isolate other parishioners who are equally traumatized. Moreover, preaching indirectly ministered to other parishioners grieving over personal losses.

Homiletic Approaches

In chapter 4, the presenter studied some general preaching themes connected with the three major events: tragic deaths, suicides, and homicides. This subsection, however, accentuates specific themes or homiletic approaches associated with individual scenarios. In some cases, homiletic approaches were presented in outline form, while in other cases they were summarized. Following is a brief description of five trauma scenarios, focusing on their respective homiletic approaches. (For more information on the scenarios, see ("Description of Scenarios.")

HOMILETIC APPROACHES IN SCENARIO ONE

In the situation involving the teenager killed in a vehicular accident, the pastor utilized the following approach. His approach was not presented in complete format or detail, only in thematic format. The pastor of this congregation preached a series of messages covering twelve weeks. Each message derived from the books of Ecclesiastes and 1 Corinthians. Preaching from these books, the pastor focused on three major themes.

First, grief is good. The emphasis was on personal grief and giving oneself permission to grieve. Since the pastor was trained in substance-abuse counseling, he understood temptations to self-medicate with illegal substances. This theme, accordingly, sought to discourage people from those temptations.

Second, there is victory through death for the believer. This theme capitalized on the assurance through salvation through scripture. The pastor's emphasis here included Christ's death, burial, and resurrection. These aspects of Jesus's life bring spiritual comfort to the believer that physical death is not final.

Scenarios	Major Areas	Homiletic Approaches
Scenario 1	Tragic Death	1. Permitting oneself to grieve 2. God's consolation 3. The adjustment process
Scenario 2	Tragic Death	1. God's peace 2. God's love 3. God's faithfulness 4. God's comfort
Scenario 3	Homicide	1. Forgiveness of others 2. God's love tempers emotions. 3. Anchored in community of faith
Scenario 4	Homicide	1. Suffering of the saints 2. Sufferings of Christ 3. Waiting on God 4. Goodness of God 5. Power of forgiveness
Scenario 5	Suicide	1. Handling personal feelings 2. Expressing feelings through prayer 3. God offers Himself rather than answers.

Table 7: This table depicts individual homiletical approaches in each scenario.

Third, there is an adjustment process following the loss of a loved one. In the messages centered on this theme, the respondent focused on two main ideas. First, he stressed the necessity of adjustment for a healthy grief progression. Second, the pastor explained when these adjustments were necessary in the mourner's grief progression (see table 7).

HOMILETIC APPROACHES IN SCENARIO TWO

In this scenario, the pastor focused on the attributes of God as themes for messages that covered around twelve weeks. Some of these approaches focused on the love of God, the peace of God, and comfort through God's Spirit. Other approaches centered on the faithfulness of God to the mourner, the presence of God in tragedies, and the closeness of God through prayer. Finally, the pastor accentuated the concept of assurance in eternal life for the believer. Using this approach, the pastor encouraged the grieving congregation that the deceased was with God.

HOMILETIC APPROACHES IN SCENARIO THREE

Comforting a congregation reeling from the homicide of one of its own, the pastor employed certain approaches. He continued with these approaches for about three weeks.

He first expounded on forgiveness as a critical element of peace. Using Matthew 18:28–33 and Colossians 3:13 as his texts, the respondent encouraged forgiveness as a means of finding personal peace. He contended that an unforgiving spirit impedes the Holy Spirit's voice.

Then, the pastor emphasizes the community of faith. Using Acts 2:46 and 2 Corinthians 8:4 as a biblical platform, the pastor focused on the community of believers. His purpose was to demonstrate that all believers are members of the whole body in Christ. As such, each believer is a minister of grace and comfort.

Finally, he focused on the power of God's love. Preaching from Philippians 1:9, the pastor expounded on the love of God as the force that tempers people's emotions. In the case of this homicide, God's love has power to confront anger before it overtakes the individual's life (see table 7).

HOMILETIC APPROACHES IN SCENARIO FOUR

Consoling a grieving congregation in the aftermath of a tragic homicide ending in the demise of a child is, needless to say, overwhelming. In this particular case, the pastor reported that he preached messages related to the event for several weeks. In particular, messages focused on the suffering of the saints, the sufferings of Christ, and how these sufferings relate to those of believers. Other dominant themes were the goodness of God, the power of forgiveness, and waiting on God. Following is an excerpt from one of the pastor's sermons on Isaiah 40. The sermon's theme is waiting on God.

I. The Announcement from Our Lord (vv.1–11)
   a. It is a Prophetic Voice.
   b. It is a Powerful Voice.
   c. It is a Profound Voice.
II. The Awesomeness of Our Lord (vv. 10–31)
   a. Behold His Shepherding.
   b. Behold His Sovereignty.
III. The Assurance from Our Lord (vv. 29–31)
   a. The assurance is weak men.
   b. The assurance is given to those who wait (see table 7).

HOMILETIC APPROACHES IN SCENARIO FIVE

Ministering to a congregation that has experienced a suicide requires intense pastoral care. Most often, the messages address the emotional dynamics of comfort, peace, and God's power in consoling the grieving. In scenario five, the pastor explained that his sermon themes derived from tough questions that parishioners asked. The pastor drew his homiletic approaches from 1 Corinthians 15:55 and John 14:1–6.

The first sermon encouraged people how to properly handle their feelings of grief. As he developed this theme, the pastor urged grieving parishioners to guard against unhealthy emotional and spiritual barriers. He also explained that answers to some tough questions may be unanswerable in this life. Faith, he continued, is trusting in God while waiting on answers to tough questions.

In the second sermon, the pastor focused on the importance of telling God how one feels rather than suppressing emotions. The respondent encouraged parishioners to express their grief and to understand that grief is actually a means of connecting with God's grace. Grief, he also explained, is not one's enemy, but one's emotional friend.

In his third message, the pastor clarified that in times of sorrow God offers Himself instead of answers. It was not that God did not have answers or purposely concealed them in order to intensify one's sorrow. Rather, God wanted His people to understand that His grace is sufficient in all life's difficult times. The pastor consoled his congregation, reminding them that Jesus conquered death and that He was their victory. A table was created to show the major homiletic approaches associated with each scenario studied (see table 7).

CHAPTER 5

The aim of chapter 4 was to identify contextual characteristics. In so doing, the chapter was divided into segments to define each characteristic. These were scenario description, demographic features, homiletic strategies, homiletic engagement of dynamics, and homiletic approaches. Each segment subsequently was designed to present information pertinent to the research questions.

This chapter finalizes results in four main areas. The first area will present the findings from the study. The second area will focus on conclusions from the research, based upon research questions. Third, this chapter will accentuate contributions of the study. The fourth area will highlight possible future research endeavors.

As stated, the purpose of this research was to study preaching as a modality of pastoral care in times of traumatic deaths. Six pastors participated in the process. All the respondents experienced untimely deaths in their congregations due to trauma. For a balanced study, three types of traumatic deaths were pursued: tragic deaths, suicides, and homicides. The study respectively studied two congregations from each category that experienced untimely deaths.

The target population of the research was local pastors who experienced tragic losses due to traumas in their congregations. From there, the process investigated how the ministers engaged these losses through interviews.

The research was subsequently guided by three empirical unknowns. The first unknown investigated the value of preaching in providing pastoral care to a congregation following a traumatic loss. The second unknown examined the extent to which preaching was utilized as a means of pastoral care. The third empirical unknown explored the relationship between pastoral care and preaching following a traumatic death in a congregation.

A review of extant literature on the subject of homiletics revealed a wide variety of topics. It was surprising to find that only a few resources addressed the specific research problem. What is more, most of the literature focused on the mechanics and theory of preaching. In terms of the context, however, the majority of the literature focusing on grief was in the context of funerals. Consequently, there is a need for more research on preaching to grief following the funeral. This shortage therefore reveals an area of homiletics requiring further research.

Discoveries during the Research

This subsection will summarize findings from studying preaching as a modality of pastoral care for congregations that have suffered deaths due to traumas. In terms of demographics, the research produced some interesting findings. The research revealed that, although all the respondents possessed formal education and previous trauma experience, not all possessed specific training. Furthermore, the research examined the amount of ministry experience the respondents possessed. Even though not all respondents possessed formal ministry-related education, their ministry experiences were invaluable resources.

As for the churches, the research illuminated four basic features. First, all the congregations experienced past traumas. Second, three out of six churches were rural, and three were urban. These contexts affected the connections these congregations shared with other churches and the amount of resources readily available. Third, three of the six congregations were multiple-staff contexts. Even though the research focused mainly on the pastors, it accounted for the shared responsibility of all staff members. Finally, all the congregations studied ranged from 40 to 450 active attendees in worship. This range fell within the delimitations of the research.

With regard to homiletic strategy, the research produced important findings related to post-trauma preaching ministry. First, all the respondents agreed on two crucial elements in preaching to congregations following a traumatic loss. Those elements were listening to the Holy Spirit and listening to one's congregants during pastoral intervention. Second, the research reported another significant piece to the homiletic strategies: homiletic components. Following traumatic losses, respondents described spiritual discernment, congregational assessment, and counseling themes as helpful guides.

Next, the research examined the dynamics of homiletic intervention. The study looked at the dominant preaching themes and tasks of homiletic intervention. Regarding themes, respondents disclosed many different themes related to suicides, homicides, and tragic deaths. Some of those themes involved comfort, peace, the community of faith, and forgiveness. The tasks of homiletic intervention, conversely, were narrowed into three main areas: mobilization of congregants, coordination of support resources, and preaching the Word.

Then, the research looked at homiletic directions. In so doing, the research highlighted the homiletic campaigns of the respondents. In terms of preaching campaigns, the study presented respondents' timing, duration, and nature of preaching. After the homiletic campaigns, the chapter emphasized the various preaching approaches of each pastor. These approaches included the various themes, scripture passages, and sermonic outlines of the respondents. Finally, the research examined the primacy of preaching. All respondents testified that preaching was the most important aspect to pastoral care. In addition, they all agreed to the supremacy of scripture in preaching.

Conclusions from the Research

In order to address the conclusions from the research in a logical manner, this subsection will discuss each empirical unknown and related research questions. The first empirical unknown inquired about the value of preaching in providing pastoral care to a congregation that has suffered a tragic loss. This unknown stemmed from the various opinions presented in the literature review regarding the importance of preaching.

The first research question, then, explored how the

preacher's theological convictions inform the task of preaching to traumatized congregations. In light of the various perspectives presented in the literature review, this research question explored how the theological convictions of local pastors informed their preaching.

The respondents at times shared similar theological convictions while at other times expressing contrasting theological convictions. One particular conviction that each respondent shared was the role of preaching. All participants reported unanimously that preaching was paramount to ministering to a grieving congregation. Likewise, they considered listening to the Holy Spirit and listening to one's congregation as key elements. All the respondents, in fact, said that the first step in their preaching directions was prayer.

Prayer, from their perspectives, was the preacher's avenue for spiritual and emotional discernment. Respondents unanimously believed that prayer is essential to the pastor's ministry. In order to know what to say and where to start preaching, the pastor must have an active prayer life. This conviction regarding the importance of an active prayer life implied that pastors must continually seek God's direction and inspiration. Moreover, respondents warned against the temptation of relying completely on one's personal experiences and training.

Another shared conviction was the importance of compassion. Compassion, the respondents agreed, is a fruit of love for people. It is most effectively conveyed through the quality of one's pastoral care, especially in times of traumatic losses. The primary means by which pastors exercised love was through preaching. Although in their estimations pastoral care was a multi-tiered system, preaching was paramount.

The second empirical unknown explored the extent to which preaching is utilized as a means of providing pastoral care and respectively explored how preaching the Word of God was important to pastoral care for grieving congregations. In response to the extent to which preaching was utilized, participants explained several theories regarding homiletic campaigns. These homiletic campaigns were timing, duration, and nature of the preaching ministry. These three different homiletic campaigns and how they were subsequently executed varied among respondents.

In respect to the second research question, respondents expressed a shared conviction regarding the importance of preaching the Bible. During the literature review, the researcher discovered that there was a wide agreement on the importance of the Word of God. When interviewing respondents, however, there were no differences of opinion regarding the importance of the Word of God to preaching. In effect, all the respondents considered that the Bible is and always remains the Word of God in respect to every aspect of human existence.

At the same time, though, there was one place where the respondents differed in terms of preaching the Word. They disagreed as to the style of preaching. By *style,* the researcher means verse-by-verse versus topical preaching styles. Although most of the respondents were steadfastly anchored to expository preaching, some were not. In fact, two respondents explained that both expository and topical preaching methods had merit.

The third research question examined how the scriptural mandate to preach informs the task of preaching to traumatized congregations. In response to this question, one pastor explained that he felt commanded by the Word of God to preach the Bible. Another pastor said that unless he preaches the Word of God, he has nothing of value to say to a grieving people. All the respondents, therefore, testified that the Word of God was their source of authority and knowledge. Demonstrating how scripture undergirds one's faith, a pastor referenced Romans 10:17, which declares, "So then faith cometh by hearing, and hearing by the Word of God."

The next empirical unknown probed the relationship between pastoral support and preaching following a tragic loss in the congregation. Supporting this empirical unknown was the fourth research question, which asked how heart attitudes influence preaching to a grieving congregation. All the respondents explained three heart attitudes that were essential to preaching to a grieving congregation. The first of these attitudes was a sense of responsibility. Preachers, they contended, must have a sense of responsibility for their people. Local church ministers are not only preachers but also undershepherds.

Another heart attitude was a sense of willingness. This implied that pastors should possess the willingness to employ whatever resources and energies necessary for effective pastoral intervention. To the respondents, this willingness also meant providing a ministry of presence when and where necessary. Intervention meant self-sacrifice without neglecting self or family. This type of intervention is a delicate process.

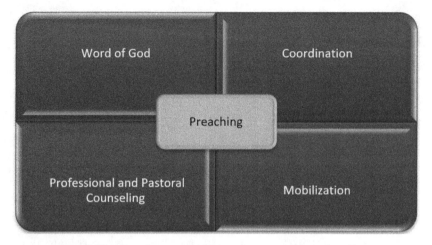

Table 8 illustrates how preaching relates to other tasks of care.

A final heart attitude was a sense of connection. Pastors must connect with their parishioners. This connection does not, however, necessarily mean understanding completely the mourner's emotions. Completely understanding another person's emotional state, one pastor noted, was impossible. Pastors can connect through listening skills and empathy.

The fifth research question, then, asked about the relationship between preaching and other tasks of pastoral care. Table 8 illustrates the tasks of pastoral intervention and how they relate to preaching. Chapter 4 described three main tasks: mobilization, coordination, and the Word of God. Pastors also explained another task related to preaching—counseling (see table 8).

Preaching, as respondents explained, inspires parishioners to respond to the grieving family in their midst. Through preaching the Word of God, people understand the sense of community they possess with each other. This sense of community among parishioners, therefore, mobilizes them to personal intervention. Preaching also emphasizes the task of coordination. One particular source that the task of preaching emphasized was small-group support. Most respondents subsequently reported that Sunday school classes were effective as internal support groups.

Likewise, one of the resources with which preaching connects people is the Bible itself. Expounding various passages illustrates how the Word of God is a source of comfort, peace, and companionship. Another source in coordination through preaching is connecting mourners with support group systems. These support groups systems may be organized within or outside the church.

In terms of the final task, pastors also agreed that preaching the Word is a form of counseling. Preaching the Word of God accentuates the Bible's inherent wisdom and relevance to all life's situations. In addition to accentuating the Bible's wisdom and relevance, preaching also illustrates the truth that in times of grief, people need support. That support might come through professional or pastoral counseling.

This research was an extensive project aimed at discovering the role of post-funeral pastoral preaching to grieving congregations. Since this research was extensive and involving various aspects, a comprehensive table that synchronizes all the aspects is presented in table 9. This table brings together the empirical unknowns, research questions, scenarios, demographic studies, and interview questions.

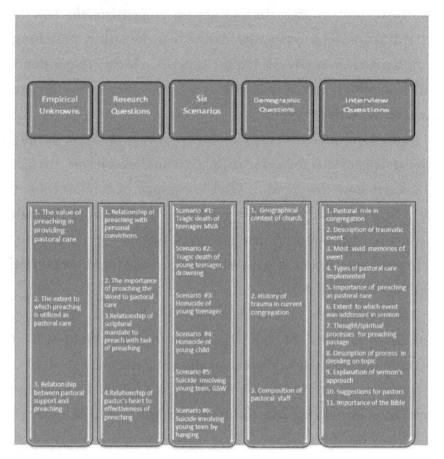

Table 9: This table synchronizes all aspects of the research.

CONTRIBUTIONS OF RESEARCH

The previous subsection presented the findings from the research. In so doing, the research also demonstrated the value of preaching to a grieving congregation. Research then summarized the extent to which preaching was implemented following a traumatic event. Next, the relationship between preaching and other tasks of pastoral care were examined. This next subsection presents contributions of the study to other pastors and is divided into three divisions: additional insights, significance of study, and suggested further research.

Additional Knowledge

Pondering the data compiled through the empirical and literature studies presented important insights. Principally, the data discovered through the literature review was compared with the data revealed in empirical studies. In so doing, data gained through literature studies was in some cases verified by empirical research. In other cases, however, the data gained through literature review was refuted. In every case, during the interviews, the respondents provided additional insights regarding preaching as a modality for pastoral care for congregations suffering from traumatic deaths. The following are some of these insights provided by respondents.

First, participants recommended that pastors must place a high premium on preaching. The literature review on this matter sometimes vacillated among different attitudes. At one end of the spectrum, authors considered preaching as an indispensable means of pastoral care. Conversely, some authors considered preaching as a dispensable tool. All respondents, however, contended that pastors are obligated to preach because they are God's undershepherds, called to preach the Word of God.

With respect to the call to preach, one respondent added a key insight. He said that pastors earn the right to preach as well as the right to have people listen. Of course acknowledging that God calls one to preach, the respondent substantiated his claim by emphasizing the importance of a trust relationship. Parishioners, he explained, must feel that they can trust their pastor's heart before they will listen to him. This trust is developed through routine interaction and engagement with parishioners.

Likewise, a respondent explained that effectiveness in pastoral ministry is focused on three concepts: consistency, competence, and compassion. The respondent furthermore explained that pastors must strive toward consistency in the form of faithfulness to the needs of parishioners. He described the pastors' biblical knowledge and spiritual maturity as essential aspects. Pastors must study the Word constantly and always devote themselves to prayer. Finally, pastors need compassion.

Another respondent presented further insight into preaching. He declared that preachers must always preach—and use words if necessary. His point in articulating this thought was that a pastor's effectiveness in ministry is conveyed through the ministry of presence. The pastor's intervention in times of traumatic death is more widely received when the pastor is physically present with his parishioners.

During the interviews, one pastor said that pastors should first preach to Jesus before preaching to parishioners. When asked to elaborate, he explained that pastors are accountable in terms of how they handle scripture in preaching. Chiefly, however, pastors are accountable to the Lord in how they handle His Word when ministering in any context. In times of traumatic loss, pastors must ensure that they are presenting a word from God for the people of God.

Significance of the Study

This study presents information that is beneficial to pastors of local congregations. Not only is the study significant to church pastors but it is also applicable to ministers from other faiths who share similar views on scripture and preaching. The concepts presented in this research, particularly in the literature review, derived from various faith traditions. Moreover, most scholars agreed that preaching serves a critical function in ministry to people mourning over deaths sustained in traumatic events. As noted, the authors consulted in the literature review represented various faiths and echoed what the empirical research discovered.

During the empirical phase of the research, the researcher studied pastors from churches ranging from 40 to 450 active parishioners. This range was established to manage the research field. The concepts and findings presented in this study, however, are relevant for pastors of congregations of any size. In point of fact, respondents testified that the lessons they imparted in the research were universal in any context. In larger congregations, for instance, pastors will face the same dynamics of grief but on a larger scale. The concepts of comfort, peace, community of faith, forgiveness, church mobilization, and coordination of intervention resources are nonetheless applicable.

Another group of clergy that benefits from the study is chaplains. Chaplains serve in various contexts, providing spiritual and emotional care similar to that of pastors. At the same time, chaplains are different from pastors in that they serve in nonreligious environments like fire departments, police departments, and the military. What is more, chaplains are held accountable to different standards and requirements that typically do not affect local church pastors. Chaplains also serve as spiritual/emotional caregivers within subcultures and, therefore, function in the pastoral role. For instance, in terms of intervention, chaplains perform tasks similar to those of local church pastors. Some of these similar tasks are mobilization, coordination of resources, counseling, and preaching. When someone dies tragically, chaplains are called upon to provide pastoral intervention.

Suggested Research

In view of the scarcity of books, published articles, and dissertations written on preaching as a modality of pastoral care in times of traumatic loss, this study is necessary. What is more, this research project uncovered an area of homiletics and pastoral care requiring further scholarly research. Research is lacking regarding the value of preaching as pastoral care for congregations that have experienced internal violence. Many congregations have experienced internal violence through shootings. Some of these events have occurred in the last five years.

A well-known church shooting event in South Carolina occurred at Emmanuel African Methodist Episcopal Church in Charleston. In June 2015, a gunman entered Emmanuel African Methodist Episcopal Church and murdered nine people, including the pastor. Then, in November 2017, another gunman entered First Baptist Church in Sutherland Springs, Texas, and killed twenty-six people. These are only two of many such tragic events that have occurred in houses of worship. Sadly, these types of events will have extensive traumatic aftereffects in people's lives for many years. Consequently, the challenge to respond is given to pastors, district superintendents, associational directors, and presbyters. In such instances, they too will face the tough questions and challenges addressed in this study.

One could conduct extensive research in three additional areas. For instance, the frightening increase of school shootings has terrorized many communities. Many church congregations, although often feeling the emotional repercussions themselves, have served as places of refuge for the mourners. Another area of research involves the death of an adult. The dynamics involving the death of a child differ from that of an adult who may be a deeply loved and respected person.

BIBLIOGRAPHY

Aland, Kurt et. al. *The Greek New Testament*. Stuttgart: Deutsche Bibelgesellshaft, 2006.

Andrew H. Weaver et. al. "Post-Traumatic Stress, Mental Health Professionals, and the Clergy: A Need for Collaboration, Training, and Research." *Journal on Traumatic Stress*, 1996: 847-56.

Bachmann, C. Charles. *Ministering to the Grief Sufferer*. Philadelphia: Fortess Press, 1964.

Barna, George. http:www.pointofview.net/viewpoints. January 22, 2016 (accessed February 2, 2016).

Begg, Derek and Prime, Allister. On Being A Pastor: Understanding Our Calling and Work. Chicago: Moody Publishers, 2004.

Buttrick, David. *A Captive Voice: The Liberation of Preaching*. Louisville: John Knox Press, 1994.

Centers for Disease Control and Prevention. January 1, 2017. https://www.cdc.gov/violenceprevention/nvdrs (accessed December 15, 2017).

Chapell, Bryan. *Christ Centered Preaching.* Grand Rapids: Baker Book House Company, 2004.

—. *The Hardest Sermons You'll Ever Have to Preach.* Nashville: Zondervan Publishing, 2011.

Claridge, Jack. *Expore Forensics.* January 6, 2016. http://www.exporeforensics.org (accessed February 1, 2016).

Collins, Gary R. *Christian Counseling.* Dallas: Wor Publishing, 1988.

Copan, Paul. *True for You But Not for Me .* Bloomington: Bethany House Publishers, 2009.

Craddock, Fred B. *Preaching.* Nashville: Abongdon Press, 1987.

Dyer, Kristi. *Journey of the Heart.* September 11, 2002. http://www.journeyofthehearts.org (accessed June 2, 2016).

Edwards, J. kent. *Deep Preaching: Creating Sermons That Go Beyond the Superficial.* Nahville: B & H Publishing Group, 2009.

Farley, Edward. *Ecclesial Reflection.* Philadelphia: Fortress Press, 1982.

Frye, John W. *Jesus As Pastor.* Grand Rapids: Zondervan Publishing House, 2000.

Gibson, Scott M. *Preaching to a Shifting Curlture.* Grand Rapids: Baker Publishing Group, 2004.

Hamilton, Donald L. *Preaching With Balance*. Ross-Shire: Christian Focus Publications, 2007.

Haseldon, Kyle. *The Urgency of Preaching*. New York: Harper and Row Publishers Inc., 1963.

Helm, David. *Expositional Preaching: How to Speak God's Word Today*. Wheaton: Crossway Publishers, 2014.

Hughes, Robert G. *A Trumpet in the Darkness: Preaching to Mourners*. Mifflintown: Sigler Press, 1997.

Largan, George. *PHDStudent.com*. January 1, 2017. http://www. phdstudent.com (accessed March 1, 2017).

Lehman, Victor D. *The Work of the Pastor*. Valley Forge: Judson Press, 2004.

Leland Ryken and Todd Wilson. *Preaching The Word: Essays on Expository Preaching*. Wheaton: Crossway Publishers, 2007.

LeRoy H. Aden and Robert G. Hughes. *Preaching God's Compassion*. Minneapolis: Augsburg Fortess Press, 2002.

Linn, Edmnd Holt. *Preaching as Counseling*. Valley Forge: The Judson Press, 1966.

MacArthur, John. *Pastoral Ministry: How to Shpeherd Biblically*. Nashville: Thomas Nelson Inc., 2005.

—. *Preaching: How to Preach Biblically*. Nashville: Thomas Neslon Inc., 2005.

---. *Rediscovering Expository Preaching.* Dallas: Word Publishing, 1992

Miller, Calvin. *Preahcing: The Art of Narrative Exposition.* Grand Rapids: Baker Publishing Group, 2006.

Molher, Albert. *Preaching: The Centrality of Scripture.* Nashville: Thomas Nelson, 2005.

National Trauma Insitute. January 1, 2017. http://www. nationaltraumainsitute.org (accessed J une 2, 2017).

Nichols, J. Randall. *The Restoring Word: Preaching as Pastoral Care.* San Francisco: Harper & and Row Publishers Inc., 1987.

Olford, Stephen F. *Anointed Expository Preaching.* Nashville: B&H Publishiing Group, 1998.

Powery, Luke A. *Spirit Speech.* Nashville: Abingdon Press, 2009.

Rhea, Homer G. *Preaching the Word Today.* Cleveland: Thomas Nelson Inc., 2002.

Robinson, Haddon W. *Biblical Preaching.* Grand Rapids: Baker Publishing Group, 2001.

Roger Alling and David J. Schlafer. *Preaching as Pastoral Care: Sermons That Work XIII.* Harrisburg: Morehouse Publishing, 2005.

Shaddix, Jim. *The passion Drivin Sermon.* Nahville: Holman Publishers, 2003.

South Carolina Emergency Management Division. January 1, 2017. http://www.scemd.org (accessed February 2, 2017).

Tautges, Paul. *Comfort The Grieving*. Grand Rapids: Zondervan Publishers, 2014.

Teikmanis, Arthur L. *Preaching and Pastoral Care*. Philadelphia: Fortess Press, 1964.

Tenney, Merril C. *John: The Gospel of Belief*. Grand Rapids: Eerdmans Publishing Company, 1988.

The Holy Bible: The New King James Version. Nashville: Holman Bible Publishers, 1996.

Theissen, Henry C. *Lectures in Systematic Theology*. Grand Rapids: Eerdmans Publishing Company, 1989.

Whiston, William. *The New Complted Works of Josephus*. Grand Rapids: Kregel Publications, 1999.

Worden, J. William. *Grief Counseling and Grief Theropy: A Handbook for Practical Mental Health Practitioner*. New York: Springer Publishing Company, 2002.

Wright, Norman H. *The New Guide to Crisis and Trauma Counseling*. Ventura: Regal Books, 2003.

CPSIA information can be obtained
at www.ICGtesting.com
Printed in the USA
BVHW080953130820
586318BV00001B/188

9 781973 696711